Shaland's
Évora & Alentejo

Shaland's Évora & Alentejo

An Illustrated Guide to Jewish History and Sites in the Portuguese Region of Alentejo and Its Capital Évora

Irene Shaland

GTA BOOKS

GTA BOOKS

Shaland's Évora

The second book in the Shaland's Portugal Series

Copyright © 2024 by Irene Shaland

All rights reserved. No part of this book may be reproduced in any form by any electronic or mechanical means including photocopying, recording, or information storage and retrieval without permission in writing from the author.

Cover by: Alex Shaland.

All photographs copyright © Alex Shaland unless otherwise credited. All rights reserved.

Paperback Edition ISBN: 979-8-9876115-4-8

Also by Irene Shaland

~ Jewish History and Travel ~
The Dao of Being Jewish and Other Stories
Shaland's Jewish Travel Guide to Malta and Corsica
Shaland's Lisbon
~ Theater and Arts ~
Tennessee Williams on the Soviet Stage
American Theater and Drama Research 1945-Present

Dedication

To Alex, my love, always and forever. You are the reason and the inspiration for everything I do.

Table of Contents

Before You Go to Portugal — 1

Brief Overview of the Sephardic History from Biblical Times to the Edicts of Expulsion — 2

The Antiquity and the Roman Period — 2

The Visigothic Period and the First Persecutions, 450-711 — 3

The Moors and the "Golden Age" of the Sefarad, 711-1492 — 4

The Beginning of the End, 1200s-1492 — 5

The Inquisition (1478) and the Edict of Expulsion (1492) — 6

Why the Portuguese Story is Different: The Tale of Three Kings — 7

The Great Sephardic Migration from Post-Expulsion Spain and Portugal — 9

The Sephardic Diaspora as a New Phenomenon in History — 10

On the Way to Évora — 12

Setúbal and Its Jewish History — 13

A Quick "Dive" into Prehistory: Cromeleque dos Almendres — 15

ÉVORA AND ALENTEJO — **17**

Évora and Its Many Faces — 19

The Roman City — 19

Roman-Not-Roman: Aqueduct or Aqueduto da Água de Prata — 20

The Heart of Évora — 21

Following the Steps of the Jews and Crypto-Jews in Évora — 26

Walking the Streets of the Former Jewish Quarter in Évora — 27

How to Recognize Crypto-Jewish Houses — 31

Évora Public Library and Jewish Connections — 35

The Fundamental Works by Great Jewish Scientists that Launched Modern Science	36
Key Achievements of the Sephardic Jewish Scientists in Portugal	39
Évora: the Birthplace of Portuguese Inquisition	40
The Saga of Two Houses: How the Inquisition Was Brought to Portugal	42
What is Alentejo?	49
The Alentejo's Rich Jewish History	49
SIDE TRIPS FROM ÉVORA:	**51**
Rediscovering the Jewish Heritage of Alentejo in Historical Towns	51
Planning your side trips	52
Portalegre	53
Where to Learn Portalegre's History	53
Searching for Portalegre Jewish Past	54
Marvão	57
Portagem	60
Portagem: The Bridge Crossed by Thousands of Spanish Jews Escaping to Portugal in 1492	61
Castelo de Vide: Town-Museum of the Sephardic Jewish History	65
Exploring the Best Preserved Jewish Quarter in Portugal with Mr. Tapadejo	69
Learning About the Tapadejo Family	73
The Ancient Synagogue of Castelo de Vide Reborn as the Museum of Jewish Experience	75
A New Museum is Coming to Castelo de Vide!	78
The Second Suggested Side Trip from Évora: Elvas and Monsaraz	80
Driving to Monsaraz	80
Monsaraz: the Crown Jewel of Alentejo and a Treasure Trove of Jewish History	81
Monsaraz: the History	82
The Jewish Narrative of Monsaraz	88

Elvas: An Unmissable Alentejo Town for a Jewish History Explorer — 95
- Jews, Jewish Quarters, and New Christians of Elvas — 97
- Exploring the Streets and Squares of Elvas Judiarias — 99
- Searching for the Crypto-Jewish Signs on Old Buildings in Elvas Jewish Quarters — 101
- The Elvas Synagogue — 103
- Elvas's World Heritage Site: the Fortifications — 105

WE ARE WHAT WE EAT: FOOD AS A MIRROR OF HISTORY — 110
- Food as a Life-and-Death Object — 111
- Portuguese Food that Reflects Iberian History — 112
- Do not Leave Portugal without Trying Pastéis de Belém! — 114
- Discovering Another Side of the Portuguese Bread Story in Castelo de Vide — 116
- Oh Bread, Glorious Portuguese Bread! — 116
- The Country of "No Waste" Cooking — 117
- The Lesson Continues — 118

Parting Words — 119

About the Author — 121

Acknowledgments

I owe a dept of gratitude to numerous entities and individuals who both inspired and enabled me to succeed in my quest to capture the Jewish narrative of Portugal.

First and foremost, I want to thank Mr. Michael Steinberger, Founder and CEO of the Jewish Heritage Alliance (JHA), an organization dedicated to introducing the largely unknown Sephardic history to diverse audiences. The JHA's brilliant programs, especially the lectures presented by Dr. Isaac Amon, Director of Academic Research and Program Development, were instrumental in sparking my interest in the story of Sefarad and strengthening my determination to delve deeper into its amazing history by traveling to Portugal to research and write this book.

Mr. Steinberger introduced me to Ruth Calvao, Member of the JHA Board, historian, and founder of Centro de Estudos Judaicos de Trás-os-Montes located in Lisbon (Center for Jewish Studies in Trás-os-Montes). Ruth became my close friend, my mentor, and my guru in all things Sephardic. In addition, she literally opened the doors for me to several archival and museum collections. My new friend also curated my efforts to build a network of subject-matter experts and Jewish leaders who would assist in my research.

My heartfelt thanks go to two key organizations within the Portuguese tourism industry that offered invaluable support: visitPortugal and the Center of Portugal Tourism.

I am grateful to the managers and professionals from the Center of Portugal Tourism. Without their organizational support, my research of Portuguese history would not have reached the depth I was able to achieve. Marli Monteiro, Executive Director, and Antonio Belo, Head of the Center's Press, Trade, and Market Research, developed a detailed itinerary and provided highly knowledgeable professional guides, excellent accommodations at historic hotels, and customary meals at the best restaurants throughout the entire region of the center of Portugal.

My special thanks go to Mr. Isaac Assor, the founder and owner of Alegretur, the number-one travel agency in Portugal that specializes in historical tourism. A Rabbi and Jewish historian, Isaac advised me on my itineraries. His Alegretur agency organized most of my travel and provided excellent guides in Lisbon, Evora, Castello de Vida, and side trips from Porto.

Recommended by Isaac Assor, Sofia Vieira, an Évora guide par excellence, was invaluable in deepening my understanding of the Jewish history of that amazing ancient town. I am very grateful to Sofia for the remarkable tour of Évora and the cooking class in her house we were privileged to attend. In Sofia's kitchen, I learned that the kind of food people eat and how they cook it becomes a mirror of their history.

Isaac Assor was also instrumental in organizing our tour of Castelo de Vide with a truly legendary man, Carolino Tapadejo. Mr. Tapadejo, a former mayor, has dedicated his life to turning his native town into a living and breathing museum of Sephardic Jewish history. It is the best-preserved Jewish quarter in Iberia. Thanks to Mr. Tapadejo and his translator, Rui Bengala, I had an unforgettable journey into Portuguese Jewish history.

Cintia Romba, a professional guide from the Tourist Information Office in Elvas, was invaluable in helping me navigate through the mostly-forgotten Jewish history of this amazing town.

I extend my sincerest thanks to the team of specialists at the Torre do Tombo (The National Archives of Portugal in Lisbon), who provided me with the extraordinary opportunity to visit this institution and witness the restoration and preservation of Inquisition records. I specifically want to mention Dr. Silvestre Lacerda, the General Director, who organized my visit; Anabella Ribeiro, the Manager; Jose Furtado, Manager of Public Relations and Information, who was my host and a guide there; and Sonia Domingos, the documents restorer, who patiently explained to me the contents of Inquisition records and showed how the manuscripts were restored and preserved.

Finally, I am deeply grateful to my dear friends and my husband Alex who selflessly dedicated their time to reading and re-reading my drafts of this book, applying their professional knowledge, excellent editorial aptitude, and superb sense of language to every page. To my first readers, proofreaders, and editors – Sandra Kramer, Robert Berk, Sophia Muchnik, and Bryte Burtis – I owe my deepest gratitude.

Irene Shaland. May 2024. Cleveland Ohio.

Before You Go to Portugal

As the author of this Guide, I think it is essential to understand the background of the Jewish story in Portugal before commencing the exploration of Évora and Alentejo on the ground. Therefore, I invite you to learn a few historical facts.

Map of Portugal.

1

Brief Overview of the Sephardic History from Biblical Times to the Edicts of Expulsion

The Iberian or Sephardic (from Sefarad, meaning Spain) Jewish narrative constitutes an integral part of not only overall Jewish history but also world history, the course of which was radically changed by what some historians call the Saga of Sefarad. Whether you travel only to south-central Portugal, like the Alentejo region and its capital, Évora, or crisscross the entire country in pursuit of Portuguese Jewish history, this Guide will assist you in learning about the greatest scientific and intellectual achievements of the Sephardic Jews.

At the same time, you will learn about massacres, riots, expulsions, and forced conversions. During your journey, you will uncover little-known stories, one at a time, and a historical trajectory of courage, strength, survival, and rebirth.

The Antiquity and the Roman Period

Historians have difficulty determining exactly when the first Jews arrived in Iberia. Biblical scholars point out that there are references in the Bible to the western Mediterranean being known to ancient Israelites. For example, around 970 BCE, King Solomon had an alliance with the King of the Phoenicians, Hiram of Tyre, and provided him with Israelite sailors. Most likely, some of the Jewish tribes, like prosperous Asher, seafaring Zebulon, and the tribe of Dan (known for its judicial wisdom), sailed with the Phoenicians, helped to colonize the Mediterranean coast and lived in the Phoenician territories. As some historians state, early Spanish-Jewish documents refer to those tribes' descendants living in Iberia.

On Rosh Hashanah, Jews read from the *Book of Jonah*, in which Jonah is commanded by God to bring a message to the sinful people of Nineveh. That city was located in ancient Assyria, across the Tigris River from modern-day Mogul in Iraq. Jonah does not want to go there, and he runs away: he takes a ship going to the Phoenician-Jewish city of Tarshish (Tartessus on the Guadalquivir River in southwestern Spain). For me personally, that sounds like compelling proof of Jews living in Iberia since Biblical times!

Jews definitely lived in Iberia during the Roman period, 218 BCE - CE 19. Josephus Flavius, a first-century CE Roman-Jewish historian, mentions Jews moving from Judea to Sefarad. The Romans called it Hispania, their name for the Iberian Peninsula.

The Visigothic Period and the First Persecutions, 450-711

The early Germanic people, the Visigoths, arrived in Iberia after the complete dissolution of the Roman Empire. The Visigothic Kingdom occupied what are now southwestern France and the Iberian Peninsula from the 5th century until the Moorish conquest in 711.

That period was marked by the first in a series of anti-Jewish laws, such as the prohibition of intermarriages (in 305), expulsion and forced conversion (in 613), affirmation of the legality of forced baptism for the very first time in history (in 633), and prohibition of all Jewish customs and traditions, such as circumcision, the celebration of holidays, and Kashrut, among numerous others (in 653). In addition, all Jews, even those who converted to Christianity, were prohibited from testifying in court.

As Benzion Netanyahu stated in his brilliant book *The Origins of the Inquisition* (Random House, 1995), the middle of the seventh century was marked by, what he calls, the "racialization of religion." Jews began to be viewed not only as people of a religion different from Christianity but also as a "race," biologically different from "pure blood" Christians.

The Moors and the "Golden Age" of the Sefarad, 711-1492

In 711, the Moors arrived from North Africa and conquered Iberia. They were the medieval Muslims, who established a great empire in the Iberian Peninsula. Called Al-Andalus, it extended from West Africa and Maghreb to what we know today as Portugal and Spain.

The Moors regarded Jews as People of the Book and treated them with tolerance and respect. Muslim rulers encouraged learning, science, and culture. Muslims, Christians, and Jews coexisted in a spirit of mutual tolerance. Jewish scholars from this period influenced European learning, and Al-Andalus became the "capital" of world Judaism. In her book *The Ornament of the World* (Bay Back Books, 2003), Maria Rosa Menocal stated: "Tolerance was an inherent aspect of Andalusian society."

This period produced such great personalities in Jewish culture as Hasdal Ibn Shaprut (915-975), a scholar, translator, and a powerful diplomat at the court of Abd Al-Rahman III; Solomon Ibn Gabirol (1021-1055), a poet and philosopher; Moses Ben Maimon, known as Maimonides (1138-1204), a medical doctor, philosopher, and the most influential Torah scholar in the Middle Ages, to name just a few.

The Beginning of the End, 1200s-1492

The 13th century started well for the Jews of Spain under King Ferdinand III of Castile, León, and Galicia (1201-1252). He understood the value Jews brought to the kingdom, and his reign is regarded by historians as a turning point in the destinies of the Iberian Jews. He appointed a Jew, Don Meier, as the chief tax collector, as well as other Jewish high-level officials.

Ferdinand III also granted a number of privileges to the Jews in several cities. For example, he allowed the Jews of Seville to retain their synagogue and presented them with four small mosques to be transformed into synagogues. Ferdinand III became the leader of the Reconquista (reconquest or liberation) movement liberating many cities in his country from the Moors. Wanting to be seen as a tolerant ruler, he called himself the "King of Three Religions."

The 14th century was marked by the Black Death, a plague that swept across Iberia and the rest of Europe (1348-1351), and that drastically changed the situation for the Jews. They were accused of poisoning wells and spreading the disease. Murderous pogroms followed from city to city and from country to country.

The worst massacre of the entire Middle Ages happened in Seville in 1391. That was an unprecedented display of Jew-hatred and violence. Over 4,000 people were killed in a short span of time. The killing spread throughout the country, and overall 50,000 to 100,000 Jews were viciously murdered in 70 towns in Spain within three months. Tens of thousands converted to Christianity.

Historians estimate that by the 1400s, one-third of the Jews in Spain were murdered, one-third fled the country, and one-third converted to Christianity. The latter became the New Christians, or *Conversos*, who turned into a new social group, despised, hated, and persecuted. The 15th century in Spain produced the "Blood Libel" with the case of the "Holy Child of Guarda" (1491) when Jews were accused of killing Christian children and using their blood to bake matzah.

The Inquisition (1478) and the Edict of Expulsion (1492)

In the 15th century, two events happened in Spain that forever changed the destiny and mentality of the Sephardic Jews. These events also marked a turning point in world history. In 1478, the Office of the Holy Inquisition was established with the feared Tomas de Torquemada (1420-1498) as the Great Inquisitor. He was obsessed with New Christians as secret Judaizers that had to be eradicated from the face of the Christian land.

In 1492, the "Most Catholic Monarchs," King Ferdinand of Aragon and Queen Isabella of Castile, liberated Spain from the Moors and captured the last Moorish stronghold, Granada. The first matter of business for them was to turn their realm into a pure Catholic country. So, they issued the infamous "Alhambra Decree," or Edict of Expulsion, which was published in March of 1492: "We, with the counsel and advice of… great noblemen of our kingdoms… resolve to order the Jews and Jewesses of our kingdoms to depart and never to return…"

Many Jews fled to the Ottoman Empire, Greece, Turkey, North Africa, and across the border to Portugal. Estimates vary, but several sources state that more than 100,000 Jews arrived in Portugal after the edict. According to historians, before the Alhambra Decree, Portugal had 32 Jewish communities. Following the edict, Jewish refugees from Spain contributed to an unprecedented growth of Jewish communities in Portugal, totaling 139.

Why the Portuguese Story is Different: The Tale of Three Kings

King João II (1455-1495, ruled 1481-1495). He is known in Portuguese history as the first "modern" monarch. According to some relatively recent and rather controversial accounts, it was King João II who sent a person, known to the world as Christopher Columbus, to the court of Ferdinand and Isabella of Spain, as a spy on a mission. Some historians think that Columbus's mission was to make the Spaniards believe that he was going to discover the sea route to India for them, but instead he gave them the Caribbean islands. (More about that in the Mafra chapter of our previous book, *Shaland's Lisbon*.)

For the Jews, King João II was a benevolent ruler who, in 1490, directed the city fathers of Lisbon to protect the Jews from the frequent and violent anti-Jewish assaults. In 1492, he allowed more than 100,000 Jews to cross the border from Spain to Portugal. They all had to pay tax for the privilege, of course. Later on, however, King João II became infamous for his persecution of newly arrived Jewish refugees. He ordered the seizure of about two thousand Jewish children from their parents and converted them to Christianity. Then, ships took the children to the island of São Tomé as settlers.

King Manuel I (1461-1521, ruled 1495-1521). Similarly to João II, his rule began with a reasonably benign attitude toward the Jews. He even released all the Jews who had been imprisoned during the reign of João II. But in 1496, he wanted to marry Infanta Isabella of Spain, daughter of the "most Catholic monarchs." In response, Ferdinand and Isabella demanded that Manuel I get rid of the Jews who lived in his kingdom.

In December 1496, Manuel I issued his Edict of Expulsion. But fearing the financial and economic collapse of his realm, he quickly changed his strategy from expulsion to forced conversion.

The Jews of Portugal, including the former refugees from Spain, were tricked into believing that – if they did not wish to convert – they could come to Lisbon with their families and possessions, and the king's ships would be waiting in the port to take them out of the country. Tens of thousands arrived, only to discover that there were no ships. These Jews were ambushed, robbed, beaten, and forcibly converted to Christianity, often just by sprinkling holy water on them. Some Jews preferred to kill their children and then themselves, but many chose life, even when that meant becoming what was called, the "New Christians." Shortly after, King Manuel I could report to his future in-laws that there were no more Jews in his kingdom.

It is hard for us today to even imagine the magnitude of that tragedy. In the 15th century, the notion of a "secular Jew" did not exist. Deprived of their religion, traditions, books, and synagogues, the forcibly converted Jews felt lost and dead inside: people without identity, strangers to the world of the living. Unlike the situation in Spain after the Edict of Expulsion, the Portuguese Jews were forced to convert without the option of leaving the country. King Manuel I closed all borders, and they stayed closed for a while. To make things worse, the New Christians, or *Conversos*, became an obsession for the next king.

King João III (1502-1557, ruled 1521-1557). He was passionate about persecuting the *Conversos*. João III earned his infamous place in history as the king who brought the Inquisition to Portugal in 1536. The worst crime for the Inquisition was Judaizing or secretly observing Jewish traditions and rituals. So, the main target of the Holy Office of Inquisition became not the Jews – there were no Jews anymore in Iberia – but the New Christians. Violent persecution of the New Christians continued for centuries. The Inquisition was abolished only in 1808 in Spain and in 1821 in Portugal.

The Great Sephardic Migration from Post-Expulsion Spain and Portugal

The following map illustrates the migration routes chosen by those Jews who decided to flee and were able to leave their home countries, where they had lived since Biblical times. They fled to more hospitable lands such as those under the Ottomans, like Greece, Turkey, and North Africa.

The Portuguese Jews were also moving to Protestant countries and cities, such as Hamburg, Rotterdam, and Amsterdam, or to the Southwest of France, like Bordeaux and Bayonne. Many went to places in the New World, such as Brazil.

The Jewish migration after 1492-97.

The Sephardic Diaspora as a New Phenomenon in History

The establishment of the Inquisition and the expulsions, first from Spain in 1492 and then from Portugal in 1496, with the latter almost immediately becoming the edict of forced conversion, split all Sephardic Jews into two very different historic groups. We can name them "those who left" and "those who stayed."

"Those who left" formed a new phenomenon: the massive Sephardic Diaspora that altered the course of history. The Sephardic Jews of the Diaspora revitalized and recreated Jewish communities in Europe, formed new communities in the New World, and developed the "Jewish

Atlantic" with trade routes that brought global trade to a previously unattainable level.

"Those who stayed" molded into a new social class, called either New Christians or *Conversos*, or in a derogatory way, *Marranos* (swine). Even generations after conversion, they still were considered Marranos and were despised and persecuted. As Alejandre Mendes stated in his 2008 book *Barros Basto, the Marrano Mirage*, (published in Portugal): "Marranos were not only exiles amongst the nations; they were exiles amongst the Jewish Nation."

After the initial forced conversions, for centuries, Marranos would be the subjects of suspicion, denunciations, arrests, tortures, and burnings. But the burnings of synagogues and Judaizers did not mean the end of Judaism. Judaism survived in secret rooms, cellars, and memories. When Jewish books were forbidden and burned, People of the Book became People of the Memory. Despite the ruthless persecutions, Crypto-Judaism (beliefs of those who were forcibly converted to Christianity, but who secretly kept their Jewish faith and traditions alive) greatly influenced the world of the Sephardim for almost four hundred years.

Now, you are fully prepared for your exploration on the ground. With this Guide in hand, you will be visiting sites to understand the lives of those who had no choice but to adapt to living in constant fear and yet kept their Jewish spirit alive.

Évora and other towns of Alentejo, which you might visit on your side trips, will gradually reveal their secrets to you, one town and one site at a time. Even if you do not plan to travel in the near future, reading this book will illuminate the history of the Sephardic Jewish people in Portugal from ancient times through today.

On the Way to Évora

To get to Évora you can drive or take either a bus or train from anywhere in Portugal. If your first stop is Lisbon, there are a few ways you can get to Évora from there. Buses are hourly, and you will arrive at the bus station on Avenida de São Sebastião, which is west of the city center. You will have to walk about ten minutes to the old city. The train station is further away, on Avenida Dr. Barahona, to the south of the center. This will be about a twenty-five-minute walk. We preferred driving.

In full disclosure, driving to Évora from Lisbon might seem annoying because of the hectic traffic and narrow one-way streets in the old town. Despite this, we think it might be the most straightforward option to get to Évora – especially with heavy suitcases! The driving distance from Lisbon to Évora is a bit over 130 kilometers, so it might take you around two hours, depending on traffic. On the bright side, you can make a few stops on the way to see more wonders of Portugal.

I can suggest at least four such sites: **Parque Natural da Arrábida** (Arrabida Natural Park) with its unparalleled natural beauty; **Quinta da Bacalhôa**, a Renaissance period estate and winery; the ancient city of **Setúbal**; and, for the aficionados of prehistory, the **megalithic sites** near Évora.

Parque Natural da Arrábida is about 40 kilometers from Lisbon via A2. The park extends conveniently into the town of Setúbal. Arrábida is often called a paradise for nature lovers and mountain enthusiasts, and this natural wonder starts on the western edge of Setúbal. The park is named after its Serra da Arrábida mountain range, and it has the only maquis ecosystems in Portugal. We learned that the maquis ecosystem usually exists in Mediterranean regions and includes numerous aromatic shrubs like rosemary, oleander, and myrtle. The beaches in the park are very peaceful, which makes them drastically different from other coastal resorts in Portugal. Most beaches in Arrábida face south, and this minimizes the effect of the Atlantic Ocean.

Quinta da Bacalhôa estate and winery are located at the northwestern point of the Arrábida Natural Park. If you are an architecture and wine lover, this place is for you! The estate is considered one of the most beautiful early 16th-century properties in Portugal. You can take a guided tour of the *quinta* (a large country house) and visit a beautiful waterside pavilion decorated with Azulejo tiles from the 15th and 16th centuries. The winery and wine-tasting sessions there are also highly popular among the visitors.

Setúbal and Its Jewish History

Setúbal is a port city located in the south-central part of the country. It is the third largest city in continental Portugal. During the times of João III (1521–1557), who brought the Inquisition to Portugal, Setúbal became an important Crypto-Jewish center. Unlike Belmonte, Carção, or other remote towns in the North, however, Setúbal's Crypto-Judaic community disappeared well before the 1900s.

The most important Jewish personality in Setúbal history was Luís Dias. He was a self-proclaimed Messiah of Setúbal. Born to poverty and without formal education, Luís Dias managed to win the devotion of numerous *Conversos* (forcibly converted Jews) and even some Christians. Local legend has it that he was a miracle worker who was known even in Lisbon.

When Dias was arrested as a heretic by the Inquisition, he could not stand the torture and confessed to all his "crimes," finally reconciling with the Church. He was released, then soon re-arrested, and burned alive along with 83 of his "heretical" followers in 1542. We learned about the power Luís Dias held over people: one of his followers was a non-Jew government official, named Gil Vaz Bugalho. Bugalho converted to Judaism in secret and even wrote a book on how Crypto-Jews, or Judaizers, should follow Jewish law. The Inquisition arrested him, and he was burned alive in 1551.

Apart from the local legends, there are no traces of the Jewish or *Conversos*' life in Setúbal. But it is worth stopping by for a quick lunch and, if you want to stretch your legs, you can enjoy a few interesting historical gems.

Igreja de São Julião, or the Church of St. Julian

This main church of the city is classified as a National Monument. It is located on the square called **Praça de Bocage** in Setúbal. The church goes back to the 1200s, but most of the architecture is in the Manueline style. Pay attention to the side portal with its trefoil arches and carved rope motifs. After the church was damaged in the 1755 earthquake and later rebuilt, the choir was given its extravagant gilded woodwork. Do not miss the beautiful 18th-century blue-and-white Azulejo tiles portraying the life of St. Julian.

If you still have some time left, drive for about 4 minutes (less than 2 km) via **Avenue Luísa Todi** and **Estrada do Castelo de São Filipe** to reach the 1582 artillery fort named, as you could have guessed, **Forte de São Filipe**. The fort was built to defend the city against the raiding Barbary pirates. If you climb on top of the wall, you will be rewarded with beautiful views of Setúbal and the Tróia Peninsula. Do not miss the Fort Chapel entirely covered with Azulejo tiles.

To reward yourself for all your historical sightseeing, you might want to drive another few minutes via **Estrada do Castelo de São Filipe** and **Avenue Luisa Todi** to reach Casa da Baia. What used to be an 18th-century mansion serves now as Setúbal's tourist office and promotional center for regional wine, sweets, and cheese. The staff there might even treat you to a free glass of Setúbal muscatel!

Some of our friends even chose to stay overnight in Setúbal on their way from Lisbon to Évora and spend most of the time hiking in Arrábida Park. We, on the other hand, opted for prehistory.

A Quick "Dive" into Prehistory: Cromeleque dos Almendres

For years, we have been fascinated by the mysterious freestanding stone structures of Menhirs and by the civilizations that created them for purposes which, to this day, are still not completely understood. Prehistoric people were most definitely attracted to the Alentejo region near Évora due to its fertile land created by three intersected river basins. There they lived, thrived, and created their enigmatic and strangely beautiful Menhirs.

At the megalithic complex called **Cromeleque dos Almendres**, these Menhirs form spectacular circles, called Cromlechs. We wanted to see the largest existing group of this kind in the Iberian Peninsula and one of the largest in Europe, called the "megalithic universe of Évora" by archeologists.

Above: The sign showing the way to Cromeleque dos Almendres.

Right: One of the largest Menhirs in Cromeleque.

The circular arrangement of Menhirs called Cromeleque.

ÉVORA AND ALENTEJO

Évora (population about 53,500 people) is a member of the association called the Rede de Judiarias de Portugal (Routes of the Sefarad), also known as the Portuguese Network of Jewish Quarters. Established by the government in

2011, the association's mandate is to preserve historical and cultural heritage related to the Jewish history of Portugal. In addition to being part of this network, Évora was also honored to become a member of the European organization called the Network of Oldest Cities in Europe.

The only city in Portugal invited to do so, Évora joined such renowned historical cities as Argos in Greece, Beziers in France, Cadiz in Spain, Colchester in the UK, Cork in Ireland, Maastricht in Holland, Rockslide in Denmark, Tongren in Belgium, and Worms in Germany.

Évora and Its Many Faces

The Roman City

The Roman period in Portugal began in the third century BCE and lasted for over seven hundred years, until the fourth century CE. Historians believe that, just like in the rest of the country, the Jews lived in Évora during the Roman times.

On the street **Alcáçova de Baixo,** at number **13**, you find the main gate leading into the Roman city, a typical **Roman arch**, renamed **Porta de Dona Isabel** centuries later. Beyond the arch was the *Mouraria*, or the Moorish Quarter. After the reconquest of Évora by Giraldo the Fearless, Moors stayed in the area but had to move outside the city walls.

The Roman Arch in Évora.

The **Largo do Conde de Vila Flor** square, used to be the Roman Forum, and there you find a Roman temple (**Templo Romano de Évora**), called the **Temple of Diana**, a World Heritage Site. We suggest visiting the square at night as well; it is otherworldly when flooded with light.

Roman temple in Évora.

Roman-Not-Roman: Aqueduct or Aqueduto da Água de Prata

These impressive multi-level arches of the aqueduct bring clean water to the city of Évora from a source almost twenty kilometers away. Originally, the aqueduct was built in the first century CE and named to honor the Roman emperor Augustus. What we see today does not go back as far. The structure was rebuilt in 1537 by the Renaissance Portuguese architect Francisco de Arruda, creator of the iconic Belém Tower in Lisbon.

Look at the aqueduct outside the city walls and then follow the imposing arches into the city. You will witness a curious transformation: the arches become almost unrecognizable because houses and shops have been constructed beneath them!

Aqueduct in Évora.

The Heart of Évora

Find **Praça do Giraldo** in the very center of the historic city. This square has been the heart of Évora for centuries, beginning with the Moors' time: their largest market was held there. It is named after the city's first governor, who liberated Évora from the Moors in 1165. You can "meet" Giraldo at the top of many lampposts in the city. He is on the horse stepping over the beheaded Moors.

Look around the square. Moorish-style, wrought-iron balconies on the buildings are perhaps the only thing that reminds us of the Moors' seven-hundred-year domination.

Giraldo Square, Évora.

Right: The city's symbol: Giraldo the Fearless, the liberator from the Moors and beloved hero of Évora.

On the north side of the square, you will see a beautiful Renaissance **Igreja de Santo Antão** (Saint Antony Church). You will find many shops and cafés around the square.

Notice the **marble fountain** in front of the Santo Antão church. The aqueduct, that you might have already seen, supplies water to this fountain. The eight fountain spouts were meant for the eight streets radiating out from the square. Several streets are located in the former Jewish Quarter.

If you need a coffee break, look for the umbrellas: you will see a popular café in the center of the square. Before

Igreja de Santo Antão on Giraldo Square, Évora.

Fountain in front of Igreja de Santo Antão, Évora.

you take a seat and order, find a **memorial plate** on the pavement close to the south side of the fountain. This plate, called Homenagem de Évora às vítimas da inquisição Portuguesa, commemorates victims of the Inquisition.

This square is where the **Portuguese Inquisition Court** was located. The place where the court building stood is marked with the memorial plate you have just found on the ground, unnoticed by most visitors.

Memorial plate, Giraldo Square, Évora.

A terrifying multitude of ferocious sentences were handed out from that now-nonexistent building over the course of almost three hundred years (1536-1821). Not many visitors know about this memorial plate. But even for those who do, it is hard to find. The outdoor café tables are often placed right on top of it.

João III, the king who brought the Inquisition to Portugal, loved Évora, and, for thirty years, he came here often and stayed for some time. Notice the **TI**, or the tourist information sign, on the **building number 73**. This is where the king's guests used to stay, most likely to attend "entertaining festivities," like burning the Judaizers and other heretics, for example.

Stop by the TI to pick up their helpful map of the historical town. Ask any agent there to mark the streets related to long-gone Jewish history on the map. We describe these streets below.

Geraldo Square is the best place to start your **travels through Jewish history of Évora** and learn about those who were the main targets of the Inquisition: not the Jews. If you remember, officially, there were no Jews in Portugal after the forced conversion of 1497. The Inquisition's role was to eradicate religious dissent only among Christians. The worst offense for the Inquisition was Judaizing, or practicing Jewish customs in secret. So, their targeted group was the New Christians. That group exemplified a new historical phenomenon: the emergence of a large, post-expulsion, post-forced conversion, social class. They were also derogatorily called *Marrano* (swine).

Even after several generations were born to Christian families, people of Jewish origin were nevertheless despised, harassed, victimized, and continuously persecuted by the Holy Office, often with the passionate assistance of enthusiastic Christian neighbors.

While you are standing in the middle of **Giraldo Square**, face **Igreja de Santo Antão** and notice a few streets going out west (left, when facing the church). Some of these streets are believed to be the area where Jews, and later New Christians, or *Conversos*, lived.

Following the Steps of the Jews and Crypto-Jews in Évora

During the Middle Ages, Évora was second only to Lisbon as an important economic center in the Kingdom of Portugal. Likewise, the Évora Jewish Quarter of that period grew to become one of the largest and richest in the country. The estimates vary, but historians think that before forced conversion, Jews constituted about 15 to 30 percent of Évora's population.

In the fourteenth century, a royal decree commanded all Portuguese Jews, in every city and village, to live separately from Christians in segregated quarters called *Judiaries*. The main purpose of this segregation was to limit the Jews' economic and financial powers and minimize their interactions with Christians. But Évora Jews made the best of the cruel circumstances and, after 1331, created the first planned neighborhood in their city!

Évora's key Jewish business interests were in commerce. But religion, philosophy, and numerous sciences, such as mathematics and astronomy, also thrived in the community. The importance of the Évora Judiaria was demonstrated by the known fact that one of the seven *ouvidorias jurídicas*, or Jewish courts, in the country was located there. Historians believe that in the 1400s, Évora Jews were prosperous enough to build, not just one, but two synagogues. The Jewish community provided all the required services, such as *mikveh* or ritual baths, schools, hospital, leprosarium, and a court of law, to name just a few.

Walking the Streets of the Former Jewish Quarter in Évora

Though there is no solid proof, most researchers believe that the Judiaria of Évora was located in the area between the two city gates: **Portas de Alconchel** and **Portas do Raimundo**.

As we were told by our wonderful guide, Sofia Vieira, today, most people in Évora are completely unaware of the rich Jewish history in their own city, let alone able to show visitors like us where the Jewish Quarter was located. Likewise, many travelers, who come to Évora from all over the world, know nothing about that.

After exploring Giraldo Square and having a short coffee break (or lunch), follow the streets that radiate west out of the square: **Rua do Tinhoso**, **Rua da Moeda**, **Rua dos Mercadores**, and some streets that cross **Rua do Raimundo**.

You will most likely notice right away the bright colors of the houses: most doors and windows are decorated with yellow and blue, and some even have bright blue lines near the foundations.

Right: Typical Alentejo colors on the houses in the former Jewish Quarter of Évora.

Rua Romão Ramalho, one of the possible borders of the Évora Judiaria.

Many Jewish merchants lived on **Rua Alcáçova de Cima**.

The author (left) and the guide (right) on Rua Alcáçova de Cima, Évora Judiaria.

The first Jewish publisher of Portugal lived on **Rua de Burgos**.

Stop for a few moments on **Rua da Moeda** (Money Street). On this street, money was printed for the first time in Évora. Look there for house number **5** and house number **77**. House number 5 is where the Judiaria gates used to be. Rabbi's house was in front of house number 77.

Rua do Burgos, Évora Judiaria.

Close view of Rua da Moeda, Évora Judiaria.

Rua da Moeda, Évora Judiaria.

Do not miss a very narrow street named **Travessa do Barão**. One of the Évora synagogues used to stand there. The synagogue entrance was where house number **18** is now. After the expulsion of the Jews, this street was given to one person: Barão Pensão Portalegre (Barão means baron).

Travessa do Barão, Évora Judiaria.

At the end of Travessa do Barão (travessa means lane) you will see the tower of the **Convento de Santa Clara** (Convent of Saint Clara). In the post-forced conversion time, the convent tower was used to keep a close watch over the newly converted Christians.

You will notice that streets in the former Jewish Quarter are very narrow and shady. They might even look to you like a labyrinth. But by walking along these picturesque streets and alleys, you feel the past Jewish history. What you need to know, of course, is where and how to find the traces of the long-gone Jews on those streets.

How to Recognize Crypto-Jewish Houses

First, look for **double doors**. Sometimes, one door is higher than the other. These are often the indications of a former Jewish home. One door served as the entrance to the business, while the second door led to the living quarters. Below are a couple of such examples.

Also, pay close attention to the **signs** carved near some doors. Now and then, you might notice a place where the *mezuzah* was located. *Mezuzah* is a small parchment scroll inscribed with the most important Hebrew prayer. It is placed in a small case fixed to the doorpost.

Above, right: Sign of the mezuzah location, former Jewish Quarter, Évora.

That served as a sign and reminder of Jewish faith. Of course, after the expulsion and forced conversion, New Christians had to remove their *mezuzot*. But the places where they used to be installed are still noticeable, like in the photo above.

Another indication of a former Jewish/Crypto-Jewish home in Évora could be a… **cruciform**.

Example of the cruciform sign near the door, former Jewish Quarter, Évora.

The cruciform, or the sign of the cross, was often used by Crypto-Jews or New Christians in Portugal. Perhaps the family in the house wanted to show to their neighbors or passersby that they were devoted to Christianity! But there was something else hidden in these crosses that only New Christians were able to recognize: for example, a letter of the word Shaddai (meaning God) or symbols of the twelve tribes of Israel. Judiarias of Portugal are the only places – that we know of – where Jews used Christian crosses, both to conceal their Judaism from enemies and to announce it to their brethren!

Look for **Gothic pointed arch portals** in the quarter. These are also signs that those houses used to belong to the Jewish residents.

Examples of the pointed arches in Évora Judiaria.

In addition, look for the plates with signs reading ***Cabido*** on several houses in the Jewish Quarter. This means that those houses were confiscated by the Inquisition.

Right: Gothic style arch in the former Judiaria of Évora.

Above: Sign on a house confiscated by Inquisition, Évora Judiaria.

Note another interesting detail: "the **Hand of Fatima**" found on many doors. Influenced by the Moorish tradition, this "Hand" was believed to provide protection for the family inside.

Right: Hand of Fatima, Évora Judiaria.

Come to the charming square **Lago dos Mercadores**. Notice a small chapel on this picturesque square: this is how New Christians wanted to demonstrate to their neighbors their devotion to Christianity.

Lago dos Mercadores, Évora Judiaria.

Évora Public Library and Jewish Connections

Head to the square named **Largo do Conde de Vila Flor**. An impressive building at number **4** is the **Évora Public Library**. Originally, this 17th-century building was intended for the Colégio dos Moços do Coro da Sé (college of the choir boys of the city cathedral). But in 1805, the Évora Archbishop donated his outstanding personal library to the Colégio and the city.

His name was Dom Frei Manuel do Cenáculo. He was a celebrated intellectual of the Portuguese Enlightenment. The Archbishop's renowned library of over 50,000 books and rare manuscripts gave the newly-born library the reputation of one of the richest collections in the country.

So, where is the Jewish connection?

The Archbishop's collection contained ancient scientific books written by great Sephardic Jewish scientists. Those books and the geniuses who wrote them played a highly important role in changing the map of the known world. Many of their inventions and mathematical charts were invaluable in giving birth to the Age of Discoveries and, thus, turning a small country like Portugal into the leader of European knowledge and wealth.

The Fundamental Works by Great Jewish Scientists that Launched Modern Science

Our guide, Sofia Vieira, a specialist in Jewish history, brought us to the Évora Public Library. Sofia helped to persuade archivists there to show us some of the precious ancient books that were written by Jewish scientists. (Read more about the Age of Discoveries and the Jewish scientists in our book *Shaland's Lisbon*.)

The author and Sofia Vieira on the way to the Évora Public Library.

I could not believe my own eyes: we were allowed to turn the pages of the books written by Abraham Zacuto and Francisco Faleiro! These works greatly advanced the scientific progress made in Portugal, even more remarkable when compared with the rest of Europe.

The author, right, and Sofia Vieira, study ancient books at Évora Public Library Archives.

Abraham, or Abraao Zacuto (1452-1515). One of the greatest among the great, Abraham Zacuto was born in Salamanca, Spain, and arrived in Lisbon in 1492 after the Edict of Expulsion. A much venerated historian, he also was a celebrated astrologer, mathematician, and a rabbi. King João II hired him as his personal astronomer. It is impossible to overstate the impact of Zacuto's inventions: the astrolabe, astronomical tables, and maritime charts, to name just a few. They were essential for the Portuguese navigational successes.

Zacuto's *The Perpetual Almanac on Celestial Motions* (or *Almanach Perpetuum Celestium Motuum*), which we were privileged to hold in our hands, is an extensive astronomical work completed in 1496. It is considered one of the most important reference materials of its time, with particular significance for oceanic navigation. Cristopher Columbus and Vasco da Gama used Zacuto's instruments and charts. Zacuto was also highly respected by King Manuel I, who allowed him to leave the country after the forced conversion and closing of the borders. Even after 500 hundred years, Abraham Zacuto continues to be venerated and admired: there is a Moon crater named Zagut in his honor.

Abraham Zacuto, *Almanach Perpetuum*.

The second book that we were privileged to hold in our hands was written by **Francisco Faleiro**. He was a Jewish cosmographer, astronomer, and mathematician from Covilhã, Portugal. (Cosmography is the part of astronomy that is concerned with the study and description of the universe). Faleiro's birthdate is not known. What we do know is that he lived and worked during the end of the fifteenth century through, possibly, the first half of the sixteenth century. Together with his brother Ruy de Faleiro, he was the principal scientific advisor and organizer of Ferdinand Magellan's circumnavigation of the globe. Francisco Faleiro is the author of *The Treatise on the Sphere and the Art of Navigation* (or *Tratado del Esphera y del Arte del Marear*), published in 1516.

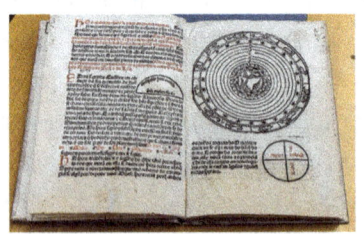

Left: Francisco Faleiro's *Guias Náutico de Évora: Tratado del Esphera y del Arte del Marear*.

After leaving the Library, we discussed the role of the Jewish scientists in the history of Portugal and that of the world. Here is a brief list of their achievements:

Key Achievements of the Sephardic Jewish Scientists in Portugal

- Made major contributions to mathematics, astronomy, cartography, medicine, philosophy, economics, and other scientific areas
- Ensured Portuguese naval supremacy
- Made possible the use of science and technology for solving navigational problems, and thus –
- Established a foundation for modern science in general and nautical science in particular

Évora: the Birthplace of Portuguese Inquisition

Begin your "mental archeological dig" into the history of the Inquisition in Évora by going to the city's twelfth-century Évora Cathedral, formally known as **Basílica Sé de Nossa Senhora da Assunção**. I would like to emphasize the importance of this house of worship: Portugal has three archbishops, and one of them resides in this cathedral. This is a remarkable building. Notice an interesting mix of styles: Romanesque transitioning to Gothic. As it happened elsewhere in Iberia, this cathedral was built on the ruins of a mosque after the country was recaptured from the Moors. The mosque, in turn, was constructed on the ruins of a Visigothic church.

Stop for a few minutes at the cathedral entrance to take a closer look at the figures of saints to your left. These victorious holy fathers stand on various symbolic interpretations of evil and heresy. There, one of the most hated evils, a Jew, is depicted as a pig.

At the entrance to Évora Cathedral: saints stand on various symbols of evil.

Évora Cathedral.

You might remember what a New Christian was called: *Marrano*, meaning swine.

Right: One of the evils, a Jew, is depicted as a swine.

What does this tell us? Long before the Inquisition was established, antisemitism, or Jew-hatred, was deeply ingrained in European consciousness and culture.

Go inside the cathedral to meet a pregnant… Virgin Mary! Midway down the nave to your left, you will find this highly unusual depiction of the beloved holy figure inside the Baroque chapel. This beautiful, fifteenth-century painted marble statue of pregnant Mary is not unique to Évora Cathedral. You will notice numerous sculptures of Mary pregnant with baby Jesus everywhere in Alentejo.

Pregnant Virgin Mary of Alentejo.

We learned that during the early years of Christianity, priests wanted to attract pagan Celtic tribes to the Church by showing God's mother as a symbol of fertility.

The Saga of Two Houses: How the Inquisition Was Brought to Portugal

After visiting the cathedral and the saints stamping out "universal evil," you are ready to follow the emergence of the Inquisition in Portugal. The Office of the Inquisition was created in Portugal in 1536 – which is 58 years after it was formed in Spain. Why then and there, and why not earlier?

Despite pogroms and massacres initiated either by the king's orders or by his intolerant Christian subjects, Kings João II and Manuel I understood the value their Jews brought to the crown. The Jewish contributions to the economy, trade, finance, sciences, and other countless areas helped to make Portugal the richest empire in Europe. King Manuel I's edict of expulsion was immediately turned into forced conversion, precisely because he wanted to keep his Jews in Portugal, but as New Christians, not as Jews.

King João III (ruled 1521-1557), however, had one obsession in his life: *Marranos*, or New Christians. Obsessing over this new evil social class among his subjects, King João III brought the Office of Inquisition into his kingdom in 1536, thus earning his infamous place in history. The Papal Bull that established the Holy Office in the Kingdom of Portugal was published in Évora in October 1536. This was the city that King João III loved and periodically lived in. And so, his beloved institution, the Inquisition, first appeared there.

To trace the steps of this loathsome history, go first to **Rua de Dona Isabel** and then turn into an alley called **Travessa das Casas Pintadas**, where you will look for house number **6**. This was the residence of the Lord of Esporão, who "engineered" the Inquisition in Portugal.

The **Lord of Esporão** served King João III as Ambassador to Madrid and Rome. He was responsible for charting the plan for establishing the Inquisition in Portugal, as well as discussing this plan with both the Pope and the Spanish Emperor Carlos V, and getting their approval.

Former House of the Lord of Esporão.

Return to **Rua Dona Isabel** and continue to **Largo do Conde de Vila** to find the former Inquisition Palace (**Palácio da Inquisição**). Completely remodeled in 2013, this sinister building received a new life as **Centro de Arte e Cultura**, or the Art and Culture Center.

The former Inquisition building.

The center focuses on contemporary arts with temporary exhibitions that are usually displayed on its two floors. Go inside, even if you are not fond of the contemporary arts.

Find the rooms with a sign reading *Gabineto do Inquisidor*, or Office of the Inquisitor.

The Author enters the former office of the Grand Inquisitor.

Inquisition insignia in one of the center's exhibition rooms.

Take a look at the ceiling. The insignia of the Inquisition is still there. The sword (symbolizing the fight against heresy) is on the right. The palm branch (symbolizing the peace the Holy Office was bringing to the world by eradicating heresy) is on the left. The Dominicans' cross is in the center.

The Holy Inquisition court in Évora was the bloodiest in the country, second only to the one in Coimbra. Most of the accusation cases for Judaizing in Portugal were processed in this building. As we were told in Évora, the number of Inquisition victims in Portugal is estimated at around 40,000. Between 1540 (the year of the first *auto-da-fé*, or the public burning of heretics) and 1794 (the year of the last public burning), tribunals in Coimbra, Évora, Lisbon, and Porto condemned over 1,175 people to burning. But some of the documentation of several *autos-da-fé* has disappeared, so these numbers are probably understated.

For King João III, the eradication of hated Judaisers was not enough. He extended the Holy Office's power over multiple aspects of Portuguese society, be it culture, politics, or even social life. He gave the Inquisitors control of censorship and allowed them to judge the "crimes" of bigamy, occultist practices, and witchcraft, to name just a few.

If the center's garden is open, do not miss it. This garden, or Jardim das Casas Pintadas, contains a real treasure: the only outside frescoes of the Renaissance period that exist in Portugal.

To complete the narrative about that infamous King João III, go to the square called **Largo da Graça**, off **Rua da República**, to find the building of the former **Church of Nossa Senhora Graça** (Grace) and the **Graça Convent**.

This remarkable complex was built in 1511 as a mausoleum for King João III. But in 1834, during the Portuguese Civil War, all monasteries and convents were abolished, and now this beautiful structure is used as Portuguese army offices. Since King João III died in the Ribeira Palace in Lisbon, he is buried in the Monastery of Jerónimos in Belém, Lisbon.

Above: Church of Nossa Senhora Graça and Graça Convent.

Right: Sculptures on the roof of the Church of Nossa Senhora Graça.

To dig deeper into the long history and culture of Évora, go to the **Museum of Évora**. It is located in another building created during the reign of King João III. Originally built as the Archiepiscopal Palace, it became a museum in 1915. The museum's rich collection of over 20,000 pieces focuses on Évora and its fascinating history.

Museum of Évora, former Archiepiscopal Palace.

The ancient city of Évora was not destroyed by the devastating earthquake of 1755 that leveled most of Lisbon. In 1986, Évora received the designation of UNESCO World Heritage Site. But with all the countless attractions of that unforgettable city, do not let your exploration of the region's Jewish history be limited to Évora only. If your time allows, treat yourself to discovering more of the **Alentejo** region, a true window into the fascinating Jewish past of Portugal.

What is Alentejo?

Alentejo means "beyond the Tagus River" in Portuguese. This region is located between the region of Algarve in the south and the central Lisbon region and occupies over one-third of the entire country. Any time you uncorked a bottle of wine, you had a chance to become acquainted with Alentejo, long before you even began to plan your trip to Portugal!

Alentejo is covered with cork oak tree forests and is the largest producer of cork in the world. When driving through Alentejo, we were surprised to see white numbers painted on cork oak trees. As we were told later, this is done with a purpose: these numbers designate the last harvest because the bark of a cork tree could be peeled only once in nine years.

Cork oak trees of Alentejo.

The Alentejo's Rich Jewish History

Just like you have discovered Judiaria in Évora, every major Alentejo town had its own Jewish quarter with synagogues, services, courts of law, and businesses. After the forced conversion of 1497 and subsequent synagogues' burnings,

Judiarias disappeared, but Judaism did not. Jews, People of the Book, many of whom had no place to escape to and chose to stay, had to become New Christians. But as you have seen on various door signs in the Évora Jewish Quarter, these Jewish *Conversos* strived to preserve their faith and traditions in secret. Without their synagogues and books, People of the Book became People of the Memory. Living in constant fear, they had the courage to preserve Judaism from generation to generation behind closed doors... and from memory.

Traveling through Alentejo, you are bound to discover that communities where Jews, and later, New Christians, lived remain an integral part of the region's history. Judiarias are remembered in place names, in *mezuzah* door slots, and in inscriptions. A persistent Jewish history seeker will find amazing traces of Alentejo's Jewish past not only in Évora but also in towns like Castelo de Vide, Elvas, Monsaraz, Marvão, and Portalegre among others.

SIDE TRIPS FROM ÉVORA:

Rediscovering the Jewish Heritage of Alentejo in Historical Towns

If your time allows, we suggest planning at least two side trips from **Évora**: the first focusing on **Castelo de Vide**, and the second focusing on **Elvas**.

We were invited to visit **Castelo de Vide** by the legendary man Carolino Tapadejo. While serving as mayor of the city, Mr. Tapadejo resurrected the fascinating Jewish past of Castelo de Vide and turned his entire town into a living historical museum, the best-preserved Jewish history town in Portugal. Carolino and a young man named Rui came to pick us up at our Évora hotel. Rui worked for the present Mayor's Office and generously agreed to be our driver and translator. On the way, our guides wanted us to also visit three amazing places, all treasure troves of history: the town of **Portalegre**, the mountaintop village of **Marvão**, and a place called **Portagem**. We advise you to do the same.

Planning your side trips

If you are driving from Lisbon, the distance to Castelo de Vide is about 225 kilometers, and it might take you about 2.5 hours via A1 and A23.

The distance from Évora to Castelo de Vide is approximately 120 kilometers along the IP2 highway, which is about a 1.5-hour drive.

If you want to start with Portalegre, like we did, driving from Évora to Portalegre will take you one hour and fifteen minutes to cover 109 km via A6 and IP2. A trip from Portalegre to Marvão is approximately 30 minutes via N359.

Portalegre, Marvão, and Portagem are very close to Castelo de Vide and are approximately 120 kilometers from Évora.

Right: Map of Portugal showing two possible side trips from Évora.

Portalegre

Where to Learn Portalegre's History

Tourist Information Center of Portalegre is located at R. Guilherme Gomes Fernandes 22, 7300-211 Portalegre, Portugal. Phone: +351-245-307-445. Open: 9:00 AM till 5:00 PM. Closed for lunch 12:30-1:30 PM. There, you can get a map of the city and ask to have places of interest marked down for you.

Today, the historical town of Portalegre has a population of approximately 16,000 and is located in the north of Alentejo, close to the Spanish border. The town is situated upland, right before the mountains of Serra de São Mamede begin to rise.

Portalegre's claim to fame is its ancient textile production tradition. During the Middle Ages this town rivaled Flanders and France as one of Europe's major textile centers. If you are interested in learning more about that famous local craft, visit the Portalegre Tapestry Museum (**Museu da Tapeçaria de Portalegre**) on **Rua da Figueira**. For history and religious art aficionados, the Municipal Museum (**Museu Municipal de Portugal**) located on **Rua José Maria da Rosa** offers its splendid collections. The museum is closed on Mondays.

Searching for Portalegre Jewish Past

When King Afonso III (1210-1279) gave Portalegre its first charter in 1259, the town was also known to cater to travelers providing them with food and shelter. The name Portalegre means "happy point," our guides told us.

According to the Questom Judaica website (https://questomjudaica.blogspot.com/2014/05/portalegre.html), by the 16th century, the Jewry of Portalegre became highly important to the Kingdom of Portugal. The amount of tax money collected from Portalegre Jewish quarters was equal to the taxes collected by the Crown in Porto and was only surpassed by Lisbon.

In search of the Jewish past, start your exploration on the central square, **Praça do Municipio**, in front of the Portalegre Cathedral (**Sé Catedral de Portalegre**).

Unfortunately for us, most of the historical center and all its major landmarks were under major reconstruction, and many buildings were covered with scaffolds. Hopefully, when you are in Portalegre, you will be able to enjoy without obstructions this town and its 16th-century baroque cathedral that seems to rule over Portalegre from its highest point.

Portalegre Cathedral is designated as a National Monument.

Look around. In the square, you see an elegant building of the Polytechnic Institute (**Instituto Politécnico de Portalegre**) and close by, a beautiful 16th-century baroque mansion, now home to the Municipal Museum (**Museu Municipal de Portalegre**).

Above: Polytechnic Institute on Praça do Municipio, Portalegre.

Right: Portalegre Municipal Museum.

Now, find the corner of **Avenue George Robinson** and **Rua de Olivença**.

Go up the steps to a small street called **Travessa do Marçal**, which leads to the part of the town where the Jews used to live. After the forced conversion of 1497, most Jewish families continued to live in the same area.

Right: Steps leading to the former Jewish Quarter.

A short walk along via **Rue de Olivença** will bring you to the square **Largo de São Lourenço** where you find the beautiful church of the same name. If the Church is open, step inside to see the interior decorated with extraordinary Azulejo tiles. While admiring the tiles, remember that you are standing on the site of the destroyed **Portalegre Synagogue**. Exit the church and walk about five minutes via **Rue de Outubro** and **Avenida da Liberdade** to reach yet another baroque church named **Espírito Santo**. Archeologists believe that this church stands on the ground where the **Jewish cemetery** used to be located.

Your Portalegre Jewish history tour is over. Return to your car and drive to Marvão.

Marvão

Locations of Portalegre, Marvão, Portagem, and Castelo de Vide on the map of Portugal.

Our guides told us that the mountainous fortress-village of Marvão has a special place in Sephardic Jewish history: being only 15 kilometers from Spain, it served as an entry point to freedom for thousands of Jews who fled Spain for Portugal after the 1492 Edict of Expulsion.

Marvão is considered one of the most beautiful places in the entire Iberian Peninsula, a miracle in the sky. Rui translated Carolino's description of the village: "Like an eagle nest hidden by the clouds." The 13th-century Marvão walls are still intact, and access to the village is only through a narrow medieval archway. Today, tiny Marvão has a population of less than one thousand people. Due to its strategic position, the village was an important point during the medieval period.

The village walls look out toward Spain on the south side and toward Serra da Estrela, Portugal, on the north side. We expected to be rewarded with great sweeping views of the two countries from the top of the Marvão walls. "If only the weather is kind to us," I thought.

Our car slowly climbed up almost three thousand feet through the icy wind and thick fog, until we reached the village of Marvão, the highest village in Portugal. We hoped the fog would clear under the sun. It was mid-April, but there was no sun, only rain, ice, wind, and the thickest fog we ever experienced. We bundled up, and, despite the cold air and freezing rain, we tried our best to enjoy the village enveloped in that strange grayish-bluish light that looked beautifully surreal.

The steep cobblestone streets were very slippery, but nevertheless, we braved the mid-April winter and walked by the whitewashed houses. Ignoring the fog, we admired wrought-iron balconies that ironically were decked with blooming flowers, all covered with ice.

Our guides told us that Marvão was founded in the 9th century by an Iberian man who converted to Islam and assumed the name Ibn-Marúan. The people of Marvão have an annual Islamic festival in October dedicated to their village founder. The festival is held jointly with the Spanish town of Badajoz across the border, also founded by the same man.

Two photos above: Inside the Marvão walls.

We decided that next time we come to Portugal, it should be in summer, and we would go to Marvão again to truly enjoy its famous beauty and iconic views.

Portagem

If the weather is nice and warm, and you like mountain hikes, you can park your car near Portagem. From there, you can climb 865 meters or 2,838 feet to Marvão. Remember, it is the highest village in Portugal! But perhaps you might prefer to drive up to Marvão and see it first, just like we did, and then drive down the mountain, arriving in twenty minutes or so in **Portagem**.

It is not a town or a village, but indeed a place near Marvão. And what a remarkable place it is! Portagem possesses a long and checkered history. The old bridge (**Ponte Velha**) you see before you was built by the Romans. "Like a giant Lego piece," our guides said, smiling. Huge granite stones were brought from the nearby Roman city of Ammaia. Still wonderfully intact, this four-arched Roman bridge marks the spot where Jews fleeing from Spain would pay a toll (*portagem* in Portuguese) to enter Portugal.

When the Jews were expelled from Spain in 1492, many of them entered Portugal via this old bridge over the Sever River (**Rio Sever**). Carolino Tapadejo's forebears, originally from Toledo, Spain, were among the refugees crossing this bridge. All exiles had to pay a toll (*portagem*). As a side note, you will see many signs reading "portagem" as you drive along the highways of Portugal: that means you will have to pay a toll up ahead.

The place where you are now is characterized by its two most notable monuments linked to the Jewish presence: the **Ponte Velha**, commonly called the **Roman Bridge**, and the medieval **Military Tower**, where the Customs House of Marvão operated.

Portagem: The Bridge Crossed by Thousands of Spanish Jews Escaping to Portugal in 1492

The view of the Portagem Bridge.

Our guides told us that, in September 1492, after the Edict of Expulsion from Spain, a Jewish refugee camp of at least 5,000 people was set up right there. The camp was guarded day and night by Portuguese soldiers to prevent the incursions of soldiers from Castille. It is estimated that out of 100,000-plus Jews entering Portugal after the edict, at least 30,000 of them crossed the border and walked over this bridge near Marvão.

Why did King João II allow so many "undesirables" to enter his realm? For a very simple reason: all refugees had to pay for the privilege of being allowed to cross the border. So, that exodus from Spain resulted in a large income for the Kingdom of Portugal.

Village near the bridge.

Side view of the ancient toll bridge, or *portagem*.

Portuguese King João II made sure that no other bridges crossing the border existed. He ordered all of them destroyed, except the one we see today. Next to the bridge, the king wanted to build a tower: a customs office of some sort. And this is where the refugees paid their toll.

Right: Toll collection tower.

In 1996 a plaque was placed on the wall of the tower in memory of the Jews who entered Portugal at this point. This plaque is the only reminder left today of the Jewish presence in Portagem.

Memorial plaque dedicated to all Jews who crossed the Portagem Bridge in 1492 looking for a safe haven in Portugal.

After you are done sightseeing, and if the weather is kind to you, you might enjoy the fantastic view from Portagem: the fortress of Marvão on the top of the mountain looks so impressively impregnable.

You might also decide to spend some time trekking along a popular route: following the 15th-century Jewish refugees' footsteps. This trek goes toward Spain, next to the Sever River. Some of our friends followed it and described the trek as "effortless" with breathtaking views along the way. It is an easy walk, they said, and the surrounding landscapes are amazing. The walk was so quiet: the only sounds they heard came from the birds and the river. I think we might take this trek as well during our next time in this area. Maybe, in the silence around us, we would hear the exiled Jews' footsteps and the crying of their children… Imagination can really take hold of you when you venture into the "mental archeology" in your quest for the past Jewish presence in Portugal…

Castelo de Vide: Town-Museum of the Sephardic Jewish History

Location of Castelo de Vide on the map of Portugal.

Located a short drive from Marvão or Portagem (a bit over 10 kilometers via N246-1), this Alentejo town is situated at the top of a mountain range called Serra do Sapoio. I am convinced that Castelo de Vide, an amazing living museum of Sephardic history, is a must-see for every traveler in search of the Portuguese Jewish past.

View of Castelo de Vide from the road.

But be warned: Castelo is also known for its steep, tortuous streets leading up to the ancient castle. Unfortunately, when we were there, that annoying icy rain just would not stop. So, we had to watch our every step!

Castelo de Vide is rather small, with its current population of less than 3,400 inhabitants. The town is a pure joy for any architecture or art aficionado. While walking the streets, we enjoyed Gothic arches, Manueline-style doorways, fountains, orchards, and the pervading smell of flowers, even during the unusually cold and rainy mid-April. The ancient stone houses seemed to be accompanying us on our walk. The entire town was surrounded by olive groves as far as the eye could see.

Afonso Henriques liberated Castelo de Vide from the Moors during the Reconquista in 1160-1166. In the 13th century, a royal charter was granted to the population, and the castle was rebuilt and extended. At that time, Castelo de Vide became strategically important for Portugal.

The Jewish presence in Castelo de Vide has been known since the 14th century. It is documented that King Pedro I (1320-1367, ruled 1357-1367) gave Mestre Lourenço, his

Centuries-old white houses on the streets of Castelo de Vide, Alentejo.

physician, who was most probably a Jew, a plot of land in Castelo de Vide. Several documents from the 15th century attest to the existence of the Jewish community there.

After the Alhambra Degree in 1492 caused a massive Jewish exodus from Spain, thousands of Jewish families came to seek refuge in Marvão and also in Castelo de Vide. Among these families were the Tapadejos from Toledo, the forebears of our friend Carolino Tapadejo.

It is believed that after 1492, between 4,000 and 5,000 Castilian Jews lived in the town. With the Spanish Jews' arrival, Castelo de Vide became an important town for commerce and manufacturing.

Following the expulsion and forced conversion in Portugal in 1496-1497, many Jewish families, including Carolino's ancestors, converted to Christianity and remained in Castelo de Vide.

Carolino Tapadejo, a local historian, former mayor, and community leader, who turned his town into a living museum of Iberian Jewish history.

Carolino shows his family heirloom: a 530-year-old key from the Tapadejo's ancestral home in Toledo, Spain. Castelo de Vide.

Now, the town of Castelo de Vide is yours to explore! Make sure to wear comfortable shoes and be ready to walk a lot!

If you are not able to arrange a meeting with Mr. Tapadejo and an accompanying translator, find the Tourist Information Office and get a map of the town and its Jewish Quarter.

Castelo de Vide Tourist Office is located on Praça D. Pedro V, 7320-123, Castelo de Vide
Tel: 245 901 361. Call in advance to confirm the working hours. Ask an agent at the TI to mark the Jewish-related streets and sites on the town map.

Exploring the Best Preserved Jewish Quarter in Portugal with Mr. Tapadejo

We began our tour at the main square named, after King Pedro V (1837-1861, ruled 1853-1861). Carolino explained that the Jews, and later those who were forced to become New Christians, lived between the square **Largo do Mercado** and the ancient **Fonte da Vila**, or village fountain. The streets of the old **Jewish Quarter** were located in the hills of Castelo de Vide, along the eastern walls of the castle.

To trace the old Judiaria, we followed Carolino from the gates of the castle down the road that led to the **Fonte da Vila** fountain, then turned onto a street called **Rua Nova**.

Above: On the way to the Old Jewish Quarter.

Left: The sign on the street where New Christians of Castelo de Vide lived.

In our travels through Portuguese Jewish history, we learned that the name **Rua Nova**, or New Street, was given to the streets where New Christians lived. That was often the same quarter where they used to live prior to forced conversion. The names of the streets, like that of **Rua Nova**, mirrored the town's Jewish history.

We also noted **Rua da Judiaria** and **Rua das Espinosas**. The latter was named after the parents of the illustrious philosopher Baruch Spinoza. They lived in town on that street after they escaped from Spain. Eventually, they were able to leave for Amsterdam, where Baruch Spinoza was born.

Street sign on Rua das Espinosas.

A street in the former Judiaria, Castelo de Vide, Alentejo.

While walking along the picturesque streets, Carolino advised us to be on the lookout for houses with special markings indicating that, centuries ago, their owners were Crypto-Jews.

We looked attentively for the signs of the long-gone Jews of Castelo de Vide. Many houses had the tell-tale double doors, just like we saw in Évora. One door led to the business owned by the family, while the other – to the stairs leading to the living quarters. We also noticed small

Former Jewish houses in Castelo de Vide.

indentations on the right doorposts of houses: Jewish families placed their *mezuzot* in those indentations. Carolino pointed to some symbols still visibly carved in

Gothic arches often indicate the former Jewish houses.

the stone wall near the doors. These symbols designated a Crypto-Jewish family, he explained, who, even after conversion, secretly practiced their faith.

Right: Carolino Tapadejo points at a sign made by Crypto-Jews. Tree of Life? Lion of Judah?

When we came to the charming **Fonte da Vila**, or the Fountain Square, we were told that this was the place where a bloody forced conversion of the entire Jewish population occurred. The charm instantly disappeared. Instead, I felt cold sweat running down my spine.

Fonte da Vila, the center of the Jewish Quarter. This fountain was the site of the forced conversion. Castelo de Vide.

Next to the fountain, you will find a white marble stele with a Jewish Star at the top. The sign in Portuguese says: "In the name of Portugal, I want to ask the persecuted Jews who were victims in our land for forgiveness." This stele was erected on March 17, 2019, at the initiative of the town mayor and the Ambassador of Israel.

It commemorates the 30th anniversary of the country's President Mario Soares asking for forgiveness for the persecution of the Jews right at the place where the violent forced conversion of the town's Jewish population took place.

Next to the stele, stands a polished grey granite stone with the inscription that reads:

Monument next to Fonte da Vila fountain.

"Shalom" to Carolino Tapadejo from the Chief Rabbi of Portugal Abraham Assor to express gratitude for all the work done by Mr. Tapadejo in preservation of the Jewish history.

Learning About the Tapadejo Family

Carolino took us to the metalworking workshop that belonged to his family for centuries. Since the end of the 15th century, the men in his family worked as metal craftsmen. Today, his son works there.

Carolino showed us the first house on **Rua do Arçário** that had an interesting story. A town's midwife lived there, we were told. In the upper window of that house, we saw a couple of brackets. Those were used for hanging out delivery sheets to report what was going on inside the house.

The workshop of the ancestors: metalworking craft persevered in the Tapadejo family over the course of five centuries.

Above: Centuries-old stamped marks of the metalworking workshop owned by Mr. Tapadejo's ancestors.

Left: The legacy is alive: Carolino proudly shows us the hammer that was used by his forebears. Castelo de Vide.

The Ancient Synagogue of Castelo de Vide Reborn as the Museum of Jewish Experience

Above and right: Going toward the synagogue, now the Museum of Jewish Experience.

At the corner of **Rua da Judiaria** and **Rua da Fonte** stands the amazing medieval synagogue of Castelo de Vide.

The building is restored to its original appearance and is reborn as the Museum of Jewish Experience. Inside you will see not only various exhibits but also the original 14th-century stone Torah ark and the *mikveh*.

The synagogue/museum consists of two floors. One of the rooms on the upper floor is believed to be the Tabernacle. Tabernacle means a "place of dwelling" or sacred confined place where G-d "dwells." The Jewish men of Castelo de Vide used to meet in this blessed small room.

Entrance to the former synagogue.

"But what about the town women?" I asked. Ladies were not forgotten, of course, explained Carolino. While the sessions of Torah studies were going on, women congregated in a space separated from their men by a small hatch. An access door to the first floor still has a small hollow for the *mezuzah*.

During the archeological examination and restoration of the ancient synagogue, the researchers discovered at least three stratigraphic levels. This finding indicated that, since the 14th century, the floor was raised at least two times. The 14th-century floor that we see today is the oldest. Surprisingly, the space was in use until the middle of the 16th century. Just to remind you: officially, there were no Jews and no Judaism in Portugal after 1497. But the building continued to be used for half a century after the forced conversion as a religious sanctuary and school. Not by Jews though, mind you, but by New Christians.

The museum exhibitions are organized thematically and chronologically: The Medieval Synagogue; The Jewish Quarter of Castelo de Vide; The Jews of Castelo de Vide and the Diaspora; Annual Celebrations and Daily Rituals; and an exhibit called In Memory of the Castelo de Vide Inhabitants – Victims of the Inquisition.

Right: Torah in the Museum of Jewish Experience, former synagogue, Castelo de Vide.

Right: Carolino shares with the author the history of the synagogue's restoration. The wall behind them lists the names of all Inquisition victims from Castelo de Vide.

Left: The signs on the Crypto-Jewish houses were created to let other New Christians know who lived in this house.

A New Museum is Coming to Castelo de Vide!

We were told that the town was going to open a new museum dedicated to the famous son of Castelo de Vide: **Garcia de Orta** (1501-1568).

The one-story house on the right is the future Garcia de Orta museum.

Garcia de Orta was born in 1501 in Castelo de Vide to a family of New Christians. He became a renowned medical doctor and a herbalist. Knowing that he might be a person of interest to the Inquisition, Garcia left for India and settled in Goa, which was a Portuguese colony at the time.

In Goa, de Orta became famous for his research in the field of tropical medicine and herbal pharmacology. There, he wrote his most renowned work about herbal pharmacology and medicine: *Colóquios dos simples e drogas da India*. Published in 1563, this treatise soon became a highly respected reference book on plant-based medicine.

By the time of de Orta's death in 1568, the Portuguese Inquisition's clutches reached Goa. Since de Orta was

Museum entrance.

already deceased, the Inquisition arrested his sister, Catarina, convicted her of Judaizing, and burned her at the stake in 1569. Under torture, she was forced to denounce her late brother. To demonstrate that even in death a heretic cannot escape the judgment of the Holy Office, the inquisitors dug up and burned de Orta's remains, along with his effigy.

Right: Memorial plaque installed by the Israeli Ambassador in 2018 in commemoration of 450 years de Orta's death.

The Second Suggested Side Trip from Évora: Elvas and Monsaraz

Driving to Monsaraz

Monsaraz is an easy drive from Évora: less than an hour (53 kilometers) via N18 and N256.
The drive time from Monsaraz to Elvas is about an hour (67 kilometers) via N373.
And, depending on traffic, you will get from Elvas back to Évora in about an hour or so (84 kilometers) via A6.

As we always suggest, have the address of the Tourist Information office (TI) in your GPS. This is where you will get your map of the historical center. Ask the person who works there to mark the sites related to Jewish history and other points of interest on the map. You will find a spacious parking lot outside the Monsaraz walls.

Tourist Information office (TI) in Monsaraz: Posto de Turismo de Monsaraz

Rua Direita 24, 7200-175, Portugal.
Tel.: +351-266-508-177

Monsaraz: the Crown Jewel of Alentejo and a Treasure Trove of Jewish History

Locations of Évora, Monsaraz, and Elvas on the map of Portugal.

Only a few places in the world that I know of preserve their ancient history with such ageless grace as the magical medieval village of Monsaraz (population less than 10,000 people). When we visited Monsaraz in April, there were almost no tourists, the sun was shining, the air was warm and full of the fragrance of flowers, and Monsaraz seemed to be whispering its secrets to us only. Or was it the echo of our lonely footsteps on the ancient village streets? For me, Monsaraz, one of the oldest villages in Portugal, seemed to be suspended in time. I believe that visiting Monsaraz is a must for any history aficionado, especially after it won the prestigious category of the Monument Village in 2017.

Before doing your usual deep dive into the Jewish stories of Monsaraz, familiarize yourself with the overall history of this unique place.

Monsaraz: the History

Historians believe that Monsaraz was already a fortified settlement in prehistoric times. This little village occupies a strategic location: situated on the top of a hill, Monsaraz offers an open view over nearby Spain.

In 1167, Geraldo Geraldes (Geraldo Sem Pavor, or Geraldo the Fearless), who you already know as the liberator of Évora, freed Monsaraz from the Moors. Shortly after, the Moors won it back, but in 1232 they were defeated by King Sancho II (1209-1248, ruled 1223-1248). Sancho II's victory was due in part to the help he received from the Knights of Templar, who assisted him in winning that historical battle. In gratitude, the king gifted this strategically-located village to the knights. (Read more about the Knights of Templar and their tragic demise in the Tomar chapter of our upcoming book dedicated to Central Portugal). Within the castle walls, you can still see some marks left by the Templars.

Now the time travel is yours!

View of Monsaraz from the parking lot.

Take a good look at the impressive stone village walls, which were especially useful during the Wars of Succession and Restoration (1640 to 1668). During these years, Monsaraz witnessed many skirmishes between Portugal and Spain.

The wall surrounding Monsaraz has four gates, and you can enter through any one of them, though the main entrance is through **Porta da Vila**, or the Village Gate. You will recognize that gate by the two semi-cylindrical towers. Look above that gate's Gothic-style arch and notice a stone dedicated to the Virgin Mary and Immaculate Conception. It was King João IV (1604-1656, ruled 1640-1656) who ordered it. That king was nicknamed "King João the Restorer" for his role during the Wars of Restoration.

If you turn your back to the gates, you will enjoy a magnificent view over the Alentejo fields.

Go inside the village walls and find the **Monsaraz Castle**. Built by King Dinis (1261-1325, ruled 1279-1325), it is now classified as a **National Monument of Portugal**.

From the top of the castle walls, you can pivot back to the 21st century by looking at the **Alqueva Dam**. This hydroelectric dam was completed in 2002, creating the largest water reservoir (or artificial lake) in Europe. We were told that this dam is considered the greatest structure of the 21st century in Portugal. Appreciative vacationers can even rent a houseboat there without any license and cruise around the lake.

Going to Monsaraz Castle.

Torre de Menagem, Castelo de Monsaraz.

Walking along the ramparts of the castle.

After admiring the **Alqueva Dam**, jump back in time five centuries and find the main square of Monsaraz, called **Largo Dom Nuno Álvares Pereira**. You will see a charming Renaissance-style church called **Igreja Matriz de Nossa Senhora da Lagoa** with a column called **Pelourinho de Monsaraz** in front of it – all shown in the next photo. We were told that the church name means Church of Our Lady of the Light. The word *pelourinho* means pillory. Placed in the central square, usually in front of the church, it was the place where criminals were bound for shaming, punishment, and exposure to public abuse.

Enter the church and find the marble tomb with 17 figures in front. Remember, it was the Knights of Templar who helped King Sancho II win Monsaraz from the Moors, and for that service, the knights received that strategic village as a "thank you" gift from the king. The tomb you are standing in front of belongs to the first *Alcaide* (Mayor) of the village. He was the Knight of Templar, and his name was Gomes Martins Silvestre. The 17 figures in front of the tomb depict the funeral procession. The past is always present in Monsaraz.

Largo Dom Nuno Álvares Pereira square and Igreja Matriz de Nossa Senhora da Lagoa church. The pillory called Pelourinho de Monsaraz is right in front of the Church.

Look to the left of **Igreja Matriz de Nossa Senhora da Lagoa**. On the corner of **Rua Direita** and a small street called **Travessa da Cadeia** you will see the entrance to **Museu do Fresco**.

The museum occupies what used to be (if we use contemporary definitions) the administrative headquarters or the town hall and the court of ancient Monsaraz. Called the **Antigos Paços da Audiência**, this building now houses a unique museum dedicated to one very special fresco. Do not miss it! This fifteenth-century fresco is called *O Bom e o Mau Juiz*, or *The Good and the Bad Judge*.

Entrance to the Museu do Fresco, Monsaraz.

What is this fresco about? On the right side of the fresco, dressed in a yellow mantle, sits the Bad Judge. How would you know that this one is "bad?" He receives bribes: partridges from the peasants (on his right) and money from the rich (on his left). In contrast, the Good Judge is dressed in angelic white robes and receives blessings from the angels.

I thought it was a great satire on the court's corruption. But as we were told, some historians believe that this most unusual fresco represents the local municipality's political struggle for the right to elect its own judges, who will of course be just and "good." The municipality was against the outsiders sent by the king. Those outsiders, of course, were corrupt and "bad." Whatever the interpretation you might choose to believe, you, most likely, just like us, would feel that it is almost impossible to leave the fresco and go outside.

When you exit the Museu do Fresco, you will find yourself inside an amazing, timeless world of charming white medieval houses and picturesque streets and alleys. Many houses have the "Hand of Fatima" door knockers, a legacy of the long-gone Moors.

Right: The "Hand of Fatima" is seen on many doors of Monsaraz.

And by now, you are about to enter the Jewish narrative of Monsaraz.

The Jewish Narrative of Monsaraz

At the intersection of **Rua de Santiago** and **Travessa da Misericórdia**, you will find **Rua Ponta da Évora** branching out to the left. On the map, this fork formed by **Rua Ponta da Évora** and **Rua de Santiago** resembles a capital letter "V". These two streets are considered the most probable location of the Jewish Quarter in the village.

At least three references point to the existence of the ancient Jewish community of Monsaraz.

First: In 1276, King Afonso III (1210-1279, ruled 1248-1279) issued a royal document that ordered the non-Christians, meaning Jews and Moors, to go to the king-appointed local judge and file charges against vicious assaults and beatings inflicted on them by the Monsaraz Christians.

Second: About three centuries later, in 1502, a curious document emerged. King Manuel I (1461-1521, ruled 1495-1521) granted a pension to the Duke of Braganza to compensate the duke for the lack of rent payments he used to receive from numerous Jewish Quarters in his lands.

Alex holds Monsaraz map to show two streets highlighted in blue that form V-shaped former Jewish neighborhood. The author stands on the street called Rua Porta de Évora.

Why wasn't the duke getting his payments anymore? The reason was simple: after King Manuel's edicts of expulsion and forced conversions (1496-1497), there were no Jews left in Portugal in general and on the "poor" duke's lands in particular. The Monsaraz Jews' share of payment was mentioned as 5,000 realis annually, a significant sum of money in those days.

Third: A document dating back to 1601 was preserved in the archives of the **Santa Casa da Misericórdia de Reguengos de Monsaraz** charity. The document stated that the former Jewish Quarter's location was within the city walls, along the streets called **Rua Porta de Évora** and **Rua de Santiago**. Of course, by that time, the former Jews had become New Christians.

If you slowly walk along one of these streets, you will find surviving traces of the past Jewish presence, like places on the wall by the door where the *mezuzah* used to be.

Right: The door with a cavity where the *mezuzah* used to be over 500 years ago, Monsaraz.

In a small place like Monsaraz, the Jews and, later, New Christians that they were forced to become, were not numerous. But they probably were of much concern to the Inquisition and troublesome enough for the Holy Office to set up the House of the Inquisitor in that tiny village.

According to the existing documentation in Torre do Tombo (National Archives) in Lisbon, there were 86 proceedings initiated against the *Maranos* of Monsaraz from 1553 through 1767. Out of these 86 proceedings, 67 were against the "Judaizers." The "concerned" neighbors denounced various heretical behaviors they observed in

Rua de Santiago in the former Monsaraz Jewish Quarter.

the nearby New Christians' homes, all related to Judaizing, or practicing Judaism in secret.

These heretical habits were documented in Inquisition folders in great detail. Among them were: sweeping the floor from the front door (where *mezuzah* used to be fixed on the doorpost) toward the interior of the house, never buying pork in the market, and lighting a candle on Friday, to mention just a few.

Casa da Inquisição, or the **House of Inquisitor**, is at the intersection of **Rua de Santiago** and **Travessa Quebra-Costas**. Today, it functions as the Interpretation Center and Museum of Local Jewish History (**Centro**

Interativo da História Judaica). Notice the sign on the wall: "This is a place of memory and a place of future… the generator of ideas for the interpretation and understanding of our history… and our identity."

This Interpretation Center is a large space dedicated to detailed and illustrated description of regional history beginning with prehistory. The local Jewish narrative is interpreted against that background. The entire center is divided into specific "chapters" that highlight the Jewish history of the village. For example, chapters include "Jewish Community of Monsaraz" and "Inquisition."

The Interpretation Center (former House of the Inquisitor).

One "chapter" specifically attracted our attention: "Dialogs of Faith." There, the curators stated: "Today our message is of a future, where the inter-religious dialog is a current practice, in which questions about faith, justice, God, and ourselves are heard and discussed…Today, Faith is no longer a shield of intolerance… Today… we all have a right to life and religious freedom."

After leaving the remarkable Interpretation Center, head to the other side of the village. On **Rua Direita**, between **Travessa do Paço** and **Rua dos Celeiros**, you will find another interesting building dating back to the 14th century, called **Casa do Juiz de Fora** (house of the judge from outside).

Rue dos Celeiros. Going to Casa do Juiz de Fora.

These judges were appointed by the king to bring royal laws to the local municipalities. The building you are looking at was indeed the residence of the village governors and "sent from the outside" judges. Today, it houses a campus of the University of Évora. Remodeled a few times during the 1500s-1600s, this building is a curious amalgamation of Gothic, Manueline, and Renaissance architectural elements.

One can easily spend an entire day in Monsaraz. But if you plan to visit Elvas as well, half a day in Monsaraz would be sufficient. It took us less than an hour to drive from Monsaraz to Elvas: 67 kilometers via N373. Put the address of the Elvas Tourist Information Office in your GPS: Praça da República 2, Elvas. Paid underground parking is conveniently located right on that square as well.

Elvas: An Unmissable Alentejo Town for a Jewish History Explorer

Praça da República, the main square of Elvas.

For your first stop in Elvas, I would recommend **Praça da República**, especially if you parked your car there. Take a good look around. Have a coffee break at a café terrace on the square: that would be a nice place to get oriented. To the north, you see the facade of Our Lady of the Assumption Cathedral (**Igreja de Nossa Senhora da Assunção**). To the south, you will find the old **Town Hall**.

Notice the beautiful square paving, called Calçada Portuguesa (a traditional Portuguese pavement). Take a closer look. This amazing stone mosaic has a modern twist: made of marble, sandstone, and basalt, the tiles are arranged in a geometric pattern to create a 3D effect!

Our Lady of the Assumption Cathedral, Praça da República, the main square of Elvas.

Looking south at Praça da República.

Get a useful city map from the Tourist Office located on the square and ask them to show you the locations of the Jewish history-related streets and sites. If Cintia Romba is still there, she would be the most helpful in the identification of the former Jewish quarters. Please show her this book and convey my best wishes and gratitude to her: Cintia

Right: Map of ancient Elvas in front of the Tourist Office.

showed us around Elvas Judiarias, was instrumental in our learning the local history, and later even followed up with her written (in Portuguese) summary.

Jews, Jewish Quarters, and New Christians of Elvas

Rarely visited by tourists, Elvas (population of about 23,000 people) is one of Portugal's hidden gems. This picturesque World Heritage town will certainly charm you with its cobblestone streets, whitewashed houses, and ancient churches. Elvas tightly guards its secrets, which you will uncover, one at a time.

Elvas's large historic center is situated within its defensive walls. This town, just like a few others you have already visited (Marvão, Castelo de Vide, Monsaraz) is strategically located. Only 12 kilometers (7 miles) from the Spanish city of Badajoz, Elvas is practically right on the border between Portugal and Spain. This location made Elvas crucial for the Portuguese military.

In 1166, during the reign of the first King of Portugal, Afonso Henriques, Elvas was liberated from the Moors for the first time. The Moors soon reconquered Elvas, but in 1229, the town was won again and incorporated into Portuguese territory by King Sancho II. The same year, King Sancho gave Elvas its first village charter.

The royal recognition of the Elvas Jewry's importance is documented in the letter "of favor" written by King Afonso V (1432-1481, ruled 1438-1481) to the local Rabbi Mestre Abraám in 1438. The king wanted this Rabbi to become responsible for all Jews in the village.

With the Edict of Expulsion of the Jews from Spain in 1492, around 10,000 Jews entered Portugal through the Badajoz-Elvas border. Some reports speak of the existence of refugee camps near the city, just like the one you learned about in Portagem near Marvão.

In 1513, King Manuel I granted a new charter to Elvas elevating the former village to the category of town. This act attests to royal recognition of Elvas's strategic and economic roles in the kingdom. At the time when the same king issued his edicts of expulsion and forced conversion, the rent paid by the Elvas Jewry to the local mayor's office amounted to 113,333 reis. The existing documents show that this sum was significantly higher than those brought in by many other Jewish communities in the kingdom.

Due to Elvas's importance for Portuguese Jewish history, this town, just like Évora, is integrated into the *Rede de Judiarias de Portugal* – the Routes of Sefarad. The documented pieces of evidence show that there was already a Jewish population in Elvas in the early 14th century. Among these documents are the 1320-1340 love songs created by a man called Vidal, a Jew from Elvas. These documents are currently preserved in the *Cancioneiro* (songbook) at the National Library in Lisbon.

The **first Jewish Quarter**, which existed from the Moorish domination period onward, was already called "old" in the 14th century. That Judiaria was located close to the center of the Muslim city. Today, this area is marked by the **Rua de Olivença** street and the nearby **Rua**

Sapateiros and **Rua Aires Varela** streets. The heart of business of that "old" Judiaria was around the street called **Rua Açougues** (previously called Rua Mercadores). The Jewish community cemetery was located outside the town walls near the **Olivença** gate.

The **"New,"** or **Nova de Elvas Judiaria**, dates back to the 14th and the 15th centuries. Its location is most probably around today's **Rua da Carreira, Rua de Olivença, Rua de Alcamim, Praça Nova, Rua da Feira**, and **Rua Carreira dos Cavalos**. Local historians believe that the "new" Jewish Quarter was situated in the upper part of the city, close to the castle and the "old" Jewish Quarter. After the forced conversion, New Christians and their descendants lived in the city area near **Rua da Feira**, close to the **Portas de Olivença** and **Porta de Évora** city gates. The **third Jewish Quarter** was located in the small town of Vila Boim located about 10 km west of Elvas via A6.

It is known that the Jews and New Christians of Elvas earned their living as merchants, goldsmiths, or apothecaries. In addition, the textile industry was highly developed in Elvas, and many Jews became tailors, fabric producers, or dealers.

In the 16th century, Elvas became an important location of the powerful Holy Office of the Portuguese Inquisition. The Inquisition there persecuted more than a thousand New Christians, thus turning Elvas into one of the most brutal towns and cities in the country.

Exploring the Streets and Squares of Elvas Judiarias

I want to point out that many streets in the old Elvas have no street signs. So, it is essential to get a map of the historic center from the Tourist Office and ask the advisors there to help you with marking the Jewish history-related sites.

Below are photos of a few streets considered to be the locations of ancient Judiaries, and they do have street signs!

Above and left: Street signs on old streets where Jews of Elvas lived centuries ago.

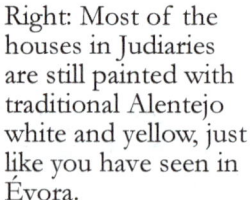

Right: Most of the houses in Judiaries are still painted with traditional Alentejo white and yellow, just like you have seen in Évora.

Manueline-style pillory in the old square, Elvas.

Our new friend from the Tourist Office, Cintia (left), tells Irene (right) to walk slowly and keep her eyes wide open.

Searching for the Crypto-Jewish Signs on Old Buildings in Elvas Jewish Quarters

Above and right: Crypto-Jewish sign of a cruciform on the gates of a house on Rua de Martim.

On **Rua de Martim Mendes**, in front of building number 20A, we saw our first Cruciform in Elvas, next to the large green metal gates leading to some government offices inside.

You can find images of cruciforms on the old walls of Elvas.

Doors with Gothic arches indicate the houses that possibly belonged to Jews or New Christians.

The Elvas Synagogue

Due to the size and economic prosperity of Elvas Jewry, there were probably not just one but at least two synagogues during the Middle Ages. But no known documents testify to the location of at least one *esnoga* (synagogue) in Elvas. Nevertheless, local historians believe that right in the heart of the "old" Jewish Quarter on **Rua dos Açougues**, several architectural elements of one restored building resemble important elements of a synagogue. For example, the twelve columns inside could be a symbol of the twelve tribes of Israel.

From the intersection of **Largo do Salvador** and **Rue dos Azevedos**, walk a few steps along **Rua dos Açougues** to **Casa da História Judaica de Elvas**.

The Largo do Salvador square is located in what used to be the "New" Judiaria in medieval Elvas.

In the 1600s, after the forced conversion, this building was repurposed as a meat market, most likely to humiliate the Jewish religion even further. Today, it houses the **Museum of Jewish History of Elvas (Casa da História**

Judaica de Elvas). Inquire at the Tourist Office when this Museum is open. You can also contact the Museum in advance. Their website is:

https://www.cm-elvas.pt/descobrir/cultura/museus/casa-da-historia-judaica/.

This building is considered to be a former synagogue. It is now the Museum of Jewish History. Rua dos Açougues, Elvas.

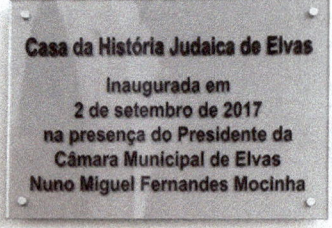

Left: Museum entrance. Above: The sign proclaims the inauguration of the Museum of Jewish History of Elvas.

Inside the Museum of Jewish History. Rua dos Açougues, Elvas.

When you complete your exploration of Elvas's Jewish past, do not leave the town yet!

Elvas's World Heritage Site: the Fortifications

Elvas's fortifications were built in the 17th century when Portugal fought Spain in the War of Restoration of Independence. Town walls were built with extended diamond-shaped ramparts, which left the attackers with no place to hide from the fire of the city defenders.

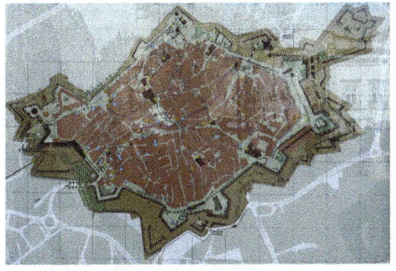

Map of ancient Elvas in front of the Tourist Office. The outer perimeter is formed by the fortifications.

Several sources state that, if the enemy managed to break through the outer walls, they would have to fight through multiple moats and narrow hidden passages designed to slow their movement. Then, the attackers would have to breach several other walls until they reached the castle.

These fortifications were built according to the design guidelines developed by Marquis de Vauban, a brilliant French military engineer of the 17th century. The Elvas castle (**Castelo de Elvas**) is located at the highest ground inside the town walls. It was originally built during the Roman times and was later used by the Moors. What you see today is the result of remodeling done in the 15th century.

Elvas Castle.

South of the town walls you will find one of the smaller forts, **Forte de Santa Luzia**. Built in the 17th century, it also has the star-shaped arrangement of the walls. During the Portuguese Liberal Wars (Guerras Liberais), this fort was used as a prison. Now it is a military museum.

View from the bell tower of Our Lady of the Assumption Cathedral. Forte de Santa Luzia can be seen behind the town walls.

Right: The Moorish Gate.

At the end of **Rua Arco do Miradeiro**, you will find the **Arch of the Miradeiro** (or the **Moorish Gate**). The gate is one of several oldest existing parts of the Elvas fortifications going back to Moorish domination. This is the original gate that formed part of the first Moorish battlements.

It was constructed using the lath and plaster building process, which was a typical Arabic technique during the

Middle Ages. This is how it worked, as we were told: The Moors used narrow strips of wood, called laths, and placed them horizontally, attaching those strips to wall studs or ceiling joists. After that, this frame was coated with plaster. The Moorish Gate also shows something else: the Roman stones! This is probably the best visual proof of the Roman period in Elvas's history.

In June 2012, UNESCO designated the historical part of Elvas and its fortifications as a World Heritage Site.

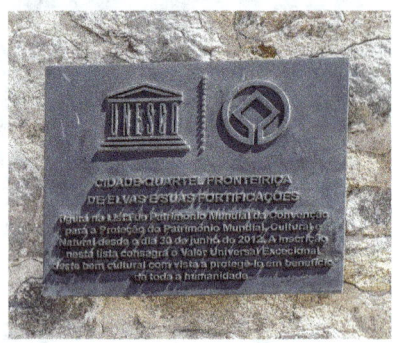

Right: UNESCO plaque mounted on the citadel wall.

Before you leave Elvas: "meet" Garcia de Orta

When you return to Praça da República to pick up your car, look for a narrow white house with a balcony. While in Castelo de Vide, you learned about Garcia de Orta, his life work, his death, and the Inquisition's revenge for dying before they could burn him alive for heresy. Now you have an opportunity to "meet" de Orta again during his youth.

The Orta family lived in Elvas on one of the streets in the old Jewish quarter. When Praça Nova, today called Praça da República, was built in 1511, some of the former Jewish houses were demolished, but the Orta family building survived. At the end of the 19th century, the ancient house was completely rebuilt, but, luckily for us Jewish history sleuths, the house retained its original doorframe.

Right: The narrow house with a balcony on Praça da República stands on the spot where the de Orta family lived.

And finally, you might want to see Elvas from above. Go to **Our Lady of the Assumption Cathedral** on the northern side of Praça da República and climb up the bell tower. The view is definitely worth the climb.

Your tour of historic Elvas ends there.

View of Elvas from the cathedral bell tower.

WE ARE WHAT WE EAT: FOOD AS A MIRROR OF HISTORY

While in Évora, we learned an important lesson at Sofia Vieira's internationally renowned Portuguese Cooking School. During our class there, watching Sofia's cooking magic and listening to her explanations, we deepened our understanding of the country's Jewish history.

In Sofia's kitchen, where she teaches her cooking classes.

Despite the edicts of expulsion and forced conversion, persecutions, and massacres, the Jewish Sephardic traditions have been forever present in Portuguese food. As Sofia explained, multiple meals that the Portuguese people cook at home and in restaurants are deeply rooted in Jewish culture. "And most people do not even suspect this," she added.

When in a restaurant, you might order a seafood stew called *caldeira* for dinner. While walking in the city, you might decide to buy a snack that looks like breaded and fried pieces of cod, called *pasteis de bacalhau*. Stopping at a café, you might order a sweet dessert, such as a spiced rice pudding called *arroz doce*. All these examples of Portuguese food are deeply rooted in Jewish Sephardic history, with some modifications, of course: Jews would never use shellfish in their "fishermen's" stews!

Food as a Life-and-Death Object

Some of the Sephardic dishes, popular even today in Portugal and Spain, were used by the Inquisition as evidence of Judaizing. In an Alentejo restaurant, we very much enjoyed our stew of lamb and fava beans with chickpeas and lots of spices. We learned from Sofia that this dish is called *adafina* and used to be a traditional meal during Shabbat.

Another dish, a sausage ubiquitous throughout Portugal, probably saved thousands of lives. Called *alheira*, this Portuguese sausage is prepared with pork; however Jews do not eat pork. After forced conversion, New Christians began preparing their sausages using the same spices as everyone else. But instead of pork, the stuffing was made either of bread, or bread mixed with chicken.

These sausages, when being cured above the fireplace, spread their aroma around the house. They looked and smelled exactly the same as those made with pork; an excellent proof of the pious faith a New Christian family needed to demonstrate to their suspicious neighbors.

Sofia Vieira shows the *alheira* sausage she stuffed with old bread and various spices.

Portuguese Food that Reflects Iberian History

Moors conquered Iberia in 711. They stayed in Portugal until the 12th-13th centuries, and in Spain through the 15th century. With them, they brought their North African (Moorish) customs and traditions that, over many centuries, deeply influenced both countries' arts, architecture, sciences, and of course, food and its preparation.

The invaders introduced almonds, figs, apricots, various citrus fruits, coriander, and cumin, to name just a few. These foods have been traditionally associated with the Portuguese southern regions of Algarve and Alentejo for centuries.

In addition, the Moors also introduced several food preservation and preparation methods. If you are traveling through Portugal – and not a vegetarian – you are bound to eat numerous salted cod (*bacalhau*) dishes. You will also see cod sold raw, salted and dried, in specialty stores. It was the Moors who brought this preservation technique to Portugal: fish or meat was salted and then dried.

Salted and dried raw cod fish.

Our favorite cod dish in Portugal was *bacalhau à Brás* (cod in the style of *Brás*), where "Brás," we were informed, might be a restaurant's name.

Right: *Bacalhau à Brás*, our favorite cod dish prepared with dried salted cod.

The dish probably has no direct connection to our topic at hand, but because it is famous throughout Portugal and, as we were told, is considered the most popular comfort meal in the country, we decided to tell you about it! *Bacalhau à Brás* has many classic ingredients found in Portuguese cooking: salted cod, eggs, shredded potatoes, and black olives.

Two other examples of the quintessential Portuguese cooking styles brought by the Moors include: breading and frying fish, and low-heat cooking of meat or fish with vegetables and spices in a closed pot. For instance, the Jewish way of cooking a *cataplana* stew was to use kosher fish with kosher white wine, garlic, tarragon, parsley, and other herbs. Kosher fish included cod, hake, mackerel, grouper, and sea bass. Cooking was done in a large pot, which made it easier to feed a large family.

In addition to the Moorish legacy that we find in Portuguese cooking, and in Sephardic cooking in particular, there is also a strong influence that came from Spain. This influence grew after over 100,000 Jews came to Portugal from Spain following the 1492 Alhambra Decree.

In numerous cafés throughout the country, we noticed familiar pastries that resembled our doughnuts from back home. "Did these come from the US?" we asked Sofia. "Oh no," she said with a laugh, "these are *pan de España* or 'bread of Spain'." She added that this type of bread has been around for more than a thousand years. Also called *pão-de-ló* (sponge cake), the recipe includes mostly eggs, sugar, and flour. Iberian Jews adapted this recipe for Passover by substituting wheat flour with matzah meal and some starch.

Do not Leave Portugal without Trying Pastéis de Belém!

Since we have already mentioned desserts like the *pão-de-ló*, we cannot help but suggest that any visitor to Portugal has, absolutely and positively, to try another one of their unique pastries: a true masterpiece called *pastéis de nata*.

These custard tarts are sold everywhere in Portugal but were invented in Belém, a suburb of Lisbon that you most likely visited while exploring the capital. So, it comes as no surprise that, in Belém, these delicious pastries are appropriately called *pastéis de Belém*, and they are the best! But remember, this pastry is not kosher and cannot be, since it includes eggs and cream.

Pastéis de nata pastries are sold everywhere in Portugal.

Bola de Berlim (translated as ball of Berlin) are displayed in the central column of the photo on the right. They look like our American doughnuts that don't have the hole in the middle. These pastries are a ubiquitous presence in cafés throughout Portugal. No Jewish connection we know of but so tasty!

Bola de Berlim (translated as ball of Berlin) are displayed in the central column of the photo.

Discovering Another Side of the Portuguese Bread Story in Castelo de Vide

When we were visiting Castelo de Vide in the Portuguese region of Alto Alentejo, our host, Mr. Carolino Tapadejo, took us to a local Jewish-style bakery. Mr. Tapadejo had his reasons to complete the Jewish story of his town and the region with a special kind of bread: *bolo finto Alentejano*.

This bread is usually made for Easter and has a very similar recipe to that of Jewish challah. Of course, challah cannot be eaten during Passover but can be enjoyed before and after the festival. So, for a New Christian family, a challah made around Easter time, adorned with brightly colored eggs for decoration and formed like *bolo finto*, might as well be a secret challah for pre- or post-Passover Shabbat!

Bolo Finto, a very special bread for Easter… and a hidden challah.

Oh Bread, Glorious Portuguese Bread!

While traveling through Alentejo, you might hear that the region is often called Cesta de Pão or the country's "bread basket." Wheat was most likely introduced to Iberia by the Romans, but it was the Moors who brought the wheat mills to Portugal. In Alentejo, Alex, who is a passionate bread aficionado, could not get enough of the customary Alentejo bread, called *pão Alentejano*, which is made with natural yeast. According to the "no waste" Portuguese tradition, this yeast is usually saved from the last bread baking.

The Country of "No Waste" Cooking

The local cooking traditions are often based on what Sofia called "nothing should be wasted" practices. This means, first and foremost, using stale bread.

In Sofia's kitchen, we participated in the process of cooking a *migas* dish, an ultimate "use-all-leftover-bread" main dish, cooked usually at the end of the week. Alex's and my contribution was to watch Sofia's every move and ask lots of questions in the process.

Sofia holds a migas dish that we all had for dinner that evening.

The word "migas" comes from the Portuguese verb "migar," or to break stale bread into crumbs. We saw migas served in restaurants and thought that it was a side dish similar to our Thanksgiving stuffing of bread crumbs and herbs; however, it is often made to look like an oval loaf, as shown in the above photo. Migas, to put it plainly, consists of bread crumbs soaked in water or kosher white wine, then mixed with olive oil, eggs, pepper, paprika, bay leaf, garlic, and lots of other herbs and spices. Some leftover shredded chicken or fish can be mixed in. Then, the mixture is rolled into an oblong loaf and cooked on medium heat in a covered pot. If small pieces of chicken or fish were not mixed in before cooking the migas, they can be placed on the plate next to it later. The incredibly appetizing aroma from this recipe was all over the kitchen!

The Lesson Continues

Sofia is preparing an appetizer: the Moroccan carrot salad.

While waiting for our migas to cook, we had a wonderful appetizer: carrot salad, another trace of the Moorish legacy. However, that dish might also have been brought to Portugal by Moroccan Sephardic Jews, who arrived in the country in the late 19th and early 20th centuries. All this salad requires is a bit of salt, black pepper, and the freshest cilantro you can find.

That was a dinner we will never forget!

Parting Words

This concludes our second book from the five-book Portuguese Jewish history series: *Shaland's Évora & Alentejo: An Illustrated Guide to Jewish History and Sites in the Portuguese Region of Alentejo and its Capital Évora.*

Both the author and the illustrator/photographer hope you found this book informative and useful. Please let us know your thoughts and suggestions by sending an email to alex.shaland.gtabooks@gmail.com.

We would also highly appreciate it if you review our book on Amazon.

So, what is next? Stay tuned for the following guides from the Portuguese series dedicated to Central Portugal, Northern Portugal, and the Azores and Madeira archipelagos.

If you sign up for Irene Shaland's Newsletter at https://globaltravelauthors.com/, you will be the first to know when each of these books becomes available!

Happy reading and happy travels!
Irene and Alex Shaland

Support for the creation of this book was provided by the following organizations and companies:

visitPortugal
Visitportugal is the official website of the national board of tourism in Portugal www.visitportugal.com/en

Center of Portugal Tourism
Center of Portugal Tourism is the official organization promoting and organizing tourism to the central part of Portugal as a spiritual and cultural center of the country. https://www.centerofportugal.com/

Alegretur
Alegretur is a tour operator specializing in religious and historical tourism. https://alegretur.com

About the Author

For Irene Shaland, globe-trotting is a passion and a way of life. She sees travel as a process of personal growth, and an opportunity to share her knowledge and experiences with readers who are enthusiastic about history, arts, and legends from the four corners of the earth. Irene and her husband Alex have visited over 90 countries and enchanted audiences with their books, magazine articles, lectures, and photography exhibits based on their travels.

Irene is an internationally published art and travel writer, Jewish historian, and educator. In her research, publications, and lectures she focuses on the rich tapestry of global Jewish experiences, culture, and heritage. Her third book, *The Dao of Being Jewish and Other Stories*, was released in 2016. Irene's new series dedicated to Jewish history travel around the world was launched in September 2021 with the publication of *Shaland's Jewish Travel Guide to Malta and Corsica: A Trusted Travel Companion for the Jewish History Explorer*.

Irene's exploration of Jewish history continues with a new five-book Portuguese series. The first book was released in December 2023: *Shaland's Lisbon: An Illustrated Guide to Jewish History and Sites in and around Lisbon*.

Irene's articles, currently numbering close to thirty, have been published in the US, Canada, the UK, France, South Africa, and Israel. A sought-after presenter, Irene lectures extensively both nationally and internationally at conferences, research centers, synagogues, art galleries, art societies, Jewish Federations, and other Jewish institutions. She is the President of the GTA Books publishing company and a founding member of the Global Travel Authors Group.

About the Photographer

Alex Shaland is the author of *Suburbanites on Safari* (2019), and a popular series of children's books *Jackie the Penguin Goes on Safari* (2022) *and Jackie the Penguin Goes to Madagascar* (2023). Alex is also an internationally published photographer. His photographs appeared in various journals and other media in the US, Canada, France, Kenya, South Korea, and the UK.

Social Media

Website: https://globaltravelauthors.com
Twitter: @ShalandGTA
Facebook:
https://www.facebook.com/GlobalTravelAuthors

BLANK PAGES FOR YOUR NOTES

www.ingramcontent.com/pod-product-compliance
Lightning Source LLC
LaVergne TN
LVHW020413070526
838199LV00054B/3604